For Reference

Not to be taken from this room

D1159957

The Isms: Modern Doctrines and Movements

Internationalism

Opposing Viewpoints

REVISED EDITION

Other Volumes Available in the *ISMS SERIES:*

The Isms: Modern Doctrines and Movements

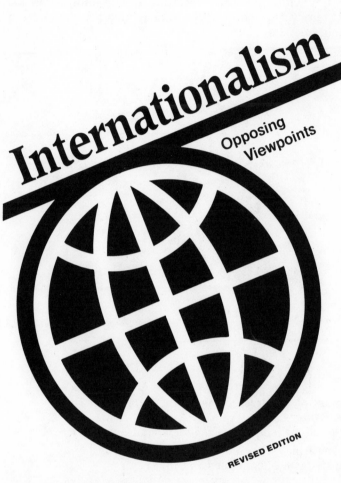

Internationalism

Opposing
Viewpoints

REVISED EDITION

Bruno Leone

Greenhaven Press

577 Shoreview Park Road
St. Paul, Minnesota 55126

Library of Congress Cataloging-in-Publication Data

Internationalism : opposing viewpoints.

(The Isms)
Includes bibliographies and index.
1. International organization—Addresses, essays, lectures. I. Leone, Bruno, 1939-   II. Series.
JX1954.I53 1986   341.2   86-339
ISBN 0-89908-383-8 (lib. bdg.)
ISBN 0-89908-358-7 (pbk.)

Second Edition
Revised

"Congress shall make no law...
abridging the freedom of speech,
or of the press."

first amendment to the U.S. Constitution

The basic foundation of our democracy is the first amendment guarantee of freedom of expression. The Opposing Viewpoints books are dedicated to the concept of this basic freedom and the idea that it is more important to practice it than to enshrine it.

Contents

Why Consider Opposing Viewpoints?

The Importance of Examining Opposing Viewpoints

The purpose of the Opposing Viewpoints books, and this book in particular, is to present balanced, and often difficult to find, opposing points of view on complex and sensitive issues.

Probably the best way to become informed is to analyze the positions of those who are regarded as experts and well studied on issues. It is important to consider every variety of opinion in an attempt to determine the truth. Opinions from the mainstream of society should be examined. But also important are opinions that are considered radical, reactionary, or minority as well as those stigmatized by some other uncomplimentary label. An important lesson of history is the eventual acceptance of many unpopular and even despised opinions. The ideas of Socrates, Jesus, and Galileo are good examples of this.

Readers will approach this book with their own opinions on the issues debated within it. However, to have a good grasp of one's own viewpoint, it is necessary to understand the arguments of those with whom one disagrees. It can be said that those who do not completely understand their adversary's point of view do not fully understand their own.

A persuasive case for considering opposing viewpoints has been presented by John Stuart Mill in his work *On Liberty*. When examining controversial issues it may be helpful to reflect on this suggestion:

> The only way in which a human being can make some approach to knowing the whole of a subject, is by hearing what can be said about it by persons of every variety of opinion, and studying all modes in which it can be looked at by every character of mind. No wise man ever acquired his wisdom in any mode but this.

Analyzing Sources of Information

The Opposing Viewpoints books include diverse materials taken from magazines, journals, books, and newspapers, as well as statements and position papers from a wide range of individuals, organizations and governments. This broad spectrum of sources helps to develop patterns of thinking which are open to the consideration of a variety of opinions.

Pitfalls to Avoid

A pitfall to avoid in considering opposing points of view is that of regarding one's own opinion as being common sense and the most rational stance and the point of view of others as being only opinion and naturally wrong. It may be that another's opinion is correct and one's own is in error.

Another pitfall to avoid is that of closing one's mind to the opinions of those with whom one disagrees. The best way to approach a dialogue is to make one's primary purpose that of understanding the mind and arguments of the other person and not that of enlightening him or her with one's own solutions. More can be learned by listening than speaking.

It is my hope that after reading this book the reader will have a deeper understanding of the issues debated and will appreciate the complexity of even seemingly simple issues on which good and honest people disagree. This awareness is particularly important in a democratic society such as ours where people enter into public debate to determine the common good. Those with whom one disagrees should not necessarily be regarded as enemies, but perhaps simply as people who suggest different paths to a common goal.

Developing Basic Reading and Thinking Skills

In this book carefully edited opposing viewpoints are purposely placed back to back to create a running debate; each viewpoint is preceded by a short quotation that best expresses the author's main argument. This format instantly plunges the reader into the midst of a controversial issue and greatly aids that reader in mastering the basic skill of recognizing an author's point of view.

A number of basic skills for critical thinking are practiced in the activities that appear throughout the books in the series. Some of the skills are:

Evaluating Sources of Information The ability to choose from among alternative sources the most reliable and accurate source in relation to a given subject.

Separating Fact from Opinion The ability to make the basic distinction between factual statements (those that can be demonstrated or verified empirically) and statements of opinion (those that are beliefs or attitudes that cannot be proved).

Identifying Stereotypes The ability to identify oversimplified, exaggerated descriptions (favorable or unfavorable) about people and insulting statements about racial, religious or national groups, based upon misinformation or lack of information.

Recognizing Ethnocentrism The ability to recognize attitudes or opinions that express the view that one's own race, culture, or group is inherently superior, or those attitudes that judge another culture or group in terms of one's own.

It is important to consider opposing viewpoints and equally important to be able to critically analyze those viewpoints. The activities in this book are designed to help the reader master these thinking skills. Statements are taken from the book's viewpoints and the reader is asked to analyze them. This technique aids the reader in developing skills that not only can be applied to the viewpoints in this book, but also to situations where opinionated spokespersons comment on controversial issues. Although the activities are helpful to the solitary reader, they are most useful when the reader can benefit from the interaction of group discussion.

Using this book and others in the series should help readers develop basic reading and thinking skills. These skills should improve the readers' ability to understand what they read. Readers should be better able to separate fact from opinion, substance from rhetoric and become better consumers of information in our media-centered culture.

This volume of the Opposing Viewpoints books does not advocate a particular point of view. Quite the contrary! The very nature of the book leaves it to the reader to formulate the opinions he or she finds most suitable. My purpose as publisher is to see that this is made possible by offering a wide range of viewpoints which are fairly presented.

David L. Bender
Publisher

Preface to
First Edition

Albert Einstein once was asked to predict how World War III would be fought. After a thoughtful pause, he responded that he could not be certain about World War III. But the war following it, he said, "will be fought with stones."

There are few who would disagree with this ominous prediction. Owing to the nature of contemporary warfare, one day some may see Einstein's opinion actualized with a prophetic vengeance.

The search for a universal and lasting peace has been humankind's most formidable quest since recorded history. And despite its desirability, peace still remains an elusive goal. One significant reason for this dilemma is the failure of most people to see beyond the narrow limits of immediate allegiances. Attachments to tribe, church, and state tend to obscure the much broader ties of a common humanity.

Internationalism is the principle which seeks to inform people of these broader ties. It may be defined as a search for a new world order based on the belief in the essential unity of humankind. Most who support the principle view it as the only viable alternative to internecine warfare.

Since ancient times, internationalism has had many articulate and devoted spokespersons. According to his biographer, W.W. Tarn, Alexander the Great "prayed for a union of hearts" among people. He dreamed of a joint commonwealth in which former enemies would live in peace. St. Augustine reminded his contemporaries that national greatness was a passing thing. For Augustine, humankind's highest goal should be to attain oneness in the universal "City of God." Dante Alighieri, best noted for his *Divine Comedy*, believed that unity was the constitutive principle of the universe. He wrote that just as the human body has one head, the world body politic also must be united under a single leader.

When the advent of gunpowder punctuated the toll and horrors of warfare, the number of internationalists increased correspondingly. And today the awful vision of Armageddon has raised the cry for international concord to a missionary fervor.

While internationalism with its promise of peace is a tempting carrot to wave before the eyes of a war-weary world, the realization of a stable global order is question of what form that unity should take. Many internationalists support a loosely knit federation of independent states cooperating, usually through an international agency, in matters of common interest. Others envision a one-world state, shorn of national boundaries and linguistic differences and both ruled and policed by a centralized executive body. There are, of course, numerous positions between these extremes.

Assuming a document of accord were promulgated, would the signatories to that agreement demonstrate the essential willingness to abide by the dictates of the majority, especially if that majority decision was deemed contrary to private national interests? The League of Nations and the United Nations are examples of the federated type of international body. Chauvinistic nationalism ultimately proved the death blow of the League, just as nationalism is seriously undermining the efficacy of the United Nations.

Harry S. Truman is quoted as saying, "Our goal must be—not peace in our time—but peace for all time." Those sentiments have been uttered by internationalists with unceasing monotony through countless periods of war and peace. And still the question remains: will internationalism ever become a true path to peace? Since history thus far has offered lamentably few favorable signs, one can only answer with the tired, worn, and familiar "only time will tell."

The following viewpoints attempt to offer a cross-section of some of the political and philosophical arguments both for and against internationalism. The reader should take careful note of the chapter on the League of Nations, as it portrays the difficulties which can arise when international interests conflict with national fears and ambitions.

Preface to Second Edition

It is with pleasure and an enormous degree of satisfaction that the second edition of Greenhaven Press's *ISMS Series: Opposing Viewpoints* has been published. The Series was so well received when it initially was made available in 1978 that plans for its revision were almost immediately formulated. During the following years, the enthusiasm of librarians and classroom teachers provided the editor with the necessary encouragement to complete the project.

While the Opposing Viewpoints format of the series has remained the same, each of the books has undergone a major revision. Because the series is developed along historical lines, materials were added or deleted in the opening chapters only where historical interpretations have changed or new sources were uncovered. The final chapters of each book have been comprehensively recast to reflect changes in the national and international situations since the original titles were published.

The Series began with six titles: *Capitalism, Communism, Internationalism, Nationalism, Racism,* and *Socialism.* A new and long overdue title, *Feminism,* has been added and several additional ones are being considered for the future. The editor offers his deepest gratitude to the dedicated and talented editorial staff of Greenhaven Press for its countless and invaluable contributions. A special thanks goes to Bonnie Szumski, whose gentle encouragement and indomitable aplomb helped carry the developing manuscripts over many inevitable obstacles. Finally, the editor thanks all future readers and hopes that the 1986 edition of the *ISMS Series* will enjoy the same reception as its predecessor.

1 CHAPTER

League of Nations

Internationalism

Introduction

At the close of World War I, twenty-seven nations gathered in Paris to negotiate the Treaty of Versailles. All hoped the treaty would settle postwar tensions. As part of the negotiations, President Woodrow Wilson presented his Fourteen Points for Peace, the last of which outlines the creation of a League of Nations as an insurance against war.

Wilson's League, however, was plagued with deficiencies from the day its members signed the treaty. First, the nations defeated in World War I were not admitted. In addition, though Wilson initiated the League himself, strong opposition in America, led largely by Senator Henry Cabot Lodge of Massachusetts and fed by a wave of American isolationism, kept the US from joining.

Without support from the US and the defeated nations, the League was powerless in preventing acts of aggression between nations. In 1923, France occupied the Ruhr and Italy occupied Kerkira, both against League pressure. In 1931, Japan invaded Manchuria and withdrew from the League. After Italy ignored League sanctions and invaded Ethiopia in 1935, the organization nearly collapsed. Finally, in 1946, it dissolved itself and transferred its Geneva headquarters to the newly formed United Nations in New York.

The following chapter attempts to illustrate the problems that plagued the League from its outset. The viewpoints range from Woodrow Wilson's impassioned plea to the American people seeking support for the League, to Benito Mussolini's nationalistic disregard for the ideals embodied in the League.

*"In the covenant of the league of nations the
moral forces of the world are mobilized."*

League of Nations:
Insurance Against War

Woodrow Wilson

The League of Nations was the brainchild of President Woodrow
Wilson. Wilson was convinced that the League represented
humankind's one hope of preventing another war of the
magnitude of World War I. Faced with the mounting congressional
opposition to America's entry into the League, he brought his case
before the electorate in a series of coast to coast speeches. Wilson
argued that it was morally imperative that the United States
become a signatory to the Covenant of the League. With typical
idealism he expressed faith in the belief that once the nations of
the world were united in an international organization dedicated
to peace, they would surely act in concert to preserve that peace.
The following viewpoint is taken from a speech the President
delivered at Pueblo, Colorado on September 25, 1919. In it, he
outlines his reasons for supporting America's entry into the
League.

As you read, consider the following questions:

1. What method did President Wilson suggest the League of
   Nations use to prevent war between belligerent nations?
2. What argument did he present to urge the United States to
   join the League of Nations?

President Woodrow Wilson in a speech delivered at Pueblo, Colorado on September 25,
1919.

The chief pleasure of my trip has been that is has nothing to do with my personal fortunes, that it has nothing to do with my personal reputation, that it has nothing to do with anything except great principles uttered by Americans of all sorts and of all parties which we are now trying to realize at this crisis of the affairs of the world. But there have been unpleasant impressions as well as pleasant impressions, my fellow citizens, as I have crossed the continent. I have perceived more and more that men have been busy creating an absolutely false impression of what the treaty of peace and the covenant of the league of nations contain and mean....

United Moral Forces of the World

At the front of this great treaty is put the covenant of the league of nations. It will also be at the front of the Austrian treaty and the Hungarian treaty and the Bulgarian treaty and the treaty with Turkey. Every one of them will contain the covenant of the league of nations, because you can not work any of them without the covenant of the league of nations. Unless you get the united, concerted purpose and power of the great Governments of the world behind this settlement, it will fall down like a house of cards. There is only one power to put behind the liberation of mankind, and that is the power of mankind. It is the power of the united moral forces of the world, and in the covenant of the league of nations the moral forces of the world are mobilized. For what purpose? Reflect, my fellow citizens, that the membership of this great league is going to include all the great fighting nations of the world, as well as the weak ones. It is not for the present going to include Germany, but for the time being Germany is not a great fighting country. All the nations that have power that can be mobilized are going to be members of this league, including the United States. And what do they unite for? They enter into a solemn promise to one another that they will never use their power against one another for aggression; that they never will impair the territorial integrity of a neighbor; that they never will interfere with the political independence of a neighbor; that they will abide by the principle that great populations are entitled to determine their own destiny and that they will not interfere with that destiny; and that no matter what differences arise amongst them they will never resort to war without first having done one or the other of two things—either submitted the matter of controversy to arbitration, in which case they agree to abide by the result without question, or submitted it to the consideration of the council of the league of nations, laying before that council all the documents, all the facts, agreeing that the council can publish the documents and the facts to the whole world, agreeing that there shall be six months allowed for the mature consideration of those facts by the council, and agreeing that at the expiration of the six months, even if they are not then ready to accept the advice of the council with regard to the settlement of the dispute, they will

20

The "Big Four" — Wilson, Orlando, Clemenceau, and Lloyd George at Versailles in 1919.

still not go to war for another three months. In other words, they consent, no matter what happens, to submit every matter of difference between them to the judgment of mankind, and just so certainly as they do that, my fellow citizens, war will be in the far background, war will be pushed out of that foreground of terror in which it has kept the world for generation after generation, and men will know that there will be a calm time of deliberate counsel. The most dangerous thing for a bad cause is to expose it to the opinion of the world. The most certain way that you can prove that a man is mistaken is by letting all his neighbors know what he thinks, by letting all his neighbors discuss what he thinks, and if he is in the wrong you will notice that he will stay at home, he will not walk on the street. He will be afraid of the eyes of his neighbors. He will be afraid of their judgment of his character. He will know that his cause is lost unless he can sustain it by the arguments of right and of justice. The same law that applies to individuals applies to nations....

I am dwelling upon these points, my fellow citizens, in spite of the fact that I dare say to most of you they are perfectly well known, because in order to meet the present situation we have got to know what we are dealing with. We are not dealing with the kind of document which this is represented by some gentlemen to be; and inasmuch as we are dealing with a document simon-pure in respect of the very principles we have professed and lived up to, we have got to do one or other of two things—we have got to adopt it or reject it. There is no middle course. You can not go in on a special-privilege basis of your own. I take it that you are too proud to ask to be exempted from responsibilities which the other members of the league will carry. We go in upon equal terms or we do not go in at all; and if we do not go in, my fellow citizens, think of the tragedy of that result—the only sufficient guaranty to the peace of the world withheld! Ourselves drawn apart with that dangerous pride which means that we shall be ready to take care of ourselves, and that means that we shall maintain great standing armies and an irresistible navy; that means we shall have the organization of a military nation; that means we shall have a general staff, with the kind of power that the general staff of Germany had, to mobilize this great manhood of the Nation when it pleases, all the energy of our young men drawn into the thought and preparation for war.

Democrats Favor League

The Democratic party favors the League of Nations as the surest, if not the only practicable means of maintaining the peace of the world and terminating the insufferable burden of great military and naval establishments. It was for this that America broke away from traditional isolation and spent her blood and treasure to crush a colossal scheme of conquest.

Democratic National Platform, 1920.

What of our pledges to the men that lie dead in France? We said that they went over there, not to prove the prowess of America or her readiness for another war but to see to it that there never was such a war again. It always seems to make it difficult for me to say anything, my fellow citizens, when I think of my clients in this case. My clients are the children; my clients are the next generation. They do not know what promises and bonds I undertook when I ordered the armies of the United States to the soil of France, but I know, and I intend to redeem my pledges, to the children; they shall not be sent upon a similar errand.

"This league is primarily...a political organization, and I object strongly to having the politics of the United States turn upon disputes where...we have no direct interest."

League of Nations: Entangling Foreign Involvement

Henry Cabot Lodge

Lawyer, historian, and US senator from Massachusetts, Henry Cabot Lodge was largely responsible for America's failure to ratify the Treaty of Versailles and gain entry into the League of Nations. As Senate Majority Leader and chairman of the Senate Committee on Foreign Relations, Lodge effectively stymied Wilson's campaign to gain popular support for admission into the League. An avowed isolationist, he later led the opposition to President Harding's plan for a World Court. In the following viewpoint, Senator Lodge lists several reasons why the US should not consider joining the League. Each of the reasons ultimately reduces to an overriding fear of foreign entanglements.

As you read, consider the following questions:

1. Why did Senator Lodge think it was in the world's best interest for the United States not to join the League?
2. What reasons did Senator Lodge advance in arguing that the United States should not join the League of Nations?

Henry Cabot Lodge in a speech delivered in the US Senate on August 12, 1919.

We ought to reduce to the lowest possible point the foreign questions in which we involve ourselves. Never forget that this league is primarily—I might say overwhelmingly—a political organization, and I object strongly to having the politics of the United States turn upon disputes where deep feeling is aroused but in which we have no direct interest. It will all tend to delay the Americanization of our great population, and it is more important not only to the United States but to the peace of the world to make all these people good Americans than it is to determine that some piece of territory should belong to one European country rather than to another. For this reason I wish to limit strictly our interference in the affairs of Europe and of Africa. We have interests of our own in Asia and in the Pacific which we must guard upon our own account, but the less we undertake to play the part of umpire and thrust ourselves into European conflicts the better for the United States and for the world.

Protect Our Independence

It has been reiterated here on this floor, and reiterated to the point of weariness, that in every treaty there is some sacrifice of sovereignty. That is not a universal truth by any means, but it is true of some treaties and it is a platitude which does not require reiteration. The question and the only question before us here is how much of our sovereignty we are justified in sacrificing. In what I have already said about other nations putting us into war I have covered one point of sovereignty which ought never to be yielded—the power to send American soldiers and sailors everywhere, which ought never to be taken from the American people or impaired in the slightest degree. Let us beware how we palter with our interdependence. We have not reached the great position from which we were able to come down into the field of battle and help to save the world from tyranny by being guided by others. Our vast power has all been built up and gathered together by ourselves alone. We forced our way upward from the days of the Revolution, through a world often hostile and always indifferent. We owe no debt to anyone except to France in that Revolution, and those policies and those rights on which our power has been founded should never be lessened or weakened. It will be no service to the world to do so and it will be of intolerable injury to the United States. We will do our share. We are ready and anxious to help in all ways to preserve the world's peace. But we can do it best by not crippling ourselves.

A Single Allegiance

I am as anxious as any human being can be to have the United States render every possible service to the civilization and the peace of mankind, but I am certain we can do it best by not putting ourselves in leading strings or subjecting our policies and our sovereignty to other nations. The interdependence of the United States is not only more precious to ourselves but to the world than any single possession....Contrast the United States with any country on the face of the earth today and ask yourself whether the situation of the United States is not the best to be found. I will go as far as anyone in the world service but the first step to world service is the maintenance of the United States. You may call me selfish, if you will, conservative or reactionary, or use any other harsh adjective you see fit to apply, but an American I was born, an American I have remained all my life. I can never be anything else

INTERRUPTING THE CEREMONY

but an American, and I must think of the United States first, and when I think of the United States first in an arrangement like this I am thinking of what is best for the world, for if the United States fails the best hopes of mankind fail with it. I have never had but one allegiance—I can not divide it now. I have loved but one flag and I can not share that devotion and give affection to the mongrel banner invented for a league. Internationalism, illustrated by the Bolshevik and by the men to whom all countries are alike provided they can make money out of them, is to me repulsive. National I must remain, and in that way I like all other Americans can render the amplest service to the world. The United States is the world's best hope, but if you fetter her in the interests and quarrels of other nations, if you tangle her in the intrigues of Europe, you will destroy her power for good and endanger her very existence. Leave her to march freely through the centuries to come as in the years that have gone....

Let the League Perish

We are told that we shall "break the heart of the world" if we do not take this league just as it stands. I fear that the hearts of the vast majority of mankind would beat on strongly and steadily and without any quickening if the league were to perish altogether. If it should be effectively and beneficiently changed the people who would lie awake in sorrow for a single night could be easily gathered in one not very large room but those who would draw a long breath of relief would reach to millions.

We hear much of visions and I trust we shall continue to have visions and dream dreams of a fairer future for the race. But visions are one thing and visionaries are another, and the mechanical appliances of the rhetorician designed to give a picture of a present which does not exist and of a future which no man can predict are as unreal and short lived as the steam or canvas clouds, the angels suspended on wires and the artificial lights of the stage. They pass with the moment of effect and are shabby and tawdry in the daylight. Let us at least be real. Washington's entire honesty of mind and his fearless look into the face of all facts are qualities which can never go out of fashion and which we should all do well to imitate.

Ideals have been thrust upon us as an argument for the league until the healthy mind which rejects can't revolt from them....

America First

No doubt many excellent and patriotic people see a coming fulfillment of noble ideals in the words "League for Peace." We all respect and share these aspirations and desires, but some of us see no hope, but rather defeat, for them in this murky covenant. For we, too, have our ideals, even if we differ from those who have tried to establish a monopoly of idealism.

26

Our first ideal is our country, and we see her in the future, as in the past, giving service to all her people and to the world. Our ideal of the future is that she should continue to render that service of her own free will. She has great problems of her own to solve, very grim and perilous problems, and a right solution, if we can attain to it, would largely benefit mankind. We would have our country

Republicans Against League

The Republican party maintains the traditional American policy of noninterference in the political affairs of other nations. This government has definitely refused membership in the League of Nations and to assume any obligations under the covenant of the League. On this we stand.

Republican National Platform, 1928.

strong to resist a peril from the West, as she has flung back the German menace from the East. We would not have our politics distracted and embittered by the dissensions of other lands. We would not have our country's vigor exhausted, or her moral force abated, by everlasting meddling and muddling in every quarrel, great and small, which afflicts the world.

"Every great international conflict will be submitted to the League of Nations as naturally as disputes between individuals are submitted to courts of law."

The League Is Working

Lord Robert Cecil

Lord Robert Cecil (1864-1958) was a British statesman who gained worldwide fame largely through his advocacy of internationalism. He was one of the earliest supporters of the League of Nations and collaborated in 1919 with President Wilson in drafting the Covenant of the League. In 1937, he was awarded the Nobel Prize for peace. The following viewpoint is taken from an address upon the League delivered by Lord Robert at the University of Geneva on September 1, 1923. In it, he explains why he believes that the League of Nations is fulfilling its purpose and expresses optimism for its future prospects.

As you read, consider the following questions:

1. What two "recent examples" does the author offer to illustrate that the League is working?
2. Why does the author believe that "too many tasks" will not over-burden the League?
3. What are some of the organized activities of the League which the author lists?

Edited from a speech delivered on September 1, 1923, at the University of Geneva, Switzerland. The speech appears in its entirety in *Living Age*, December 15, 1923.

The League of Nations is formally established; it is an international reality. Its Council and its Assembly convene at regular intervals to perform their duties. It is no longer a hope, an ideal, but an actual thing. The solidity of its foundations has been proved in more than one way, and not the least of these, in my opinion, is the growing custom of submitting to it every difficulty that arises, every question that demands an impartial inquiry.

The League Works

I shall cite two very recent examples. The Treaty of Lausanne has just been signed. I have studied this document carefully, and I have discovered that in several places it provides for an appeal to the League of Nations. If any difficult question is to be settled, such as the control of an international railway, there is a resort to the League. If a great ocean route calls for international control, in order that it may always be open to commerce, as in the case of the Dardanelles, it is provided that the International Commission in charge shall appeal to the League of Nations in case of controversy. When a solution was sought for the frontier puzzle created by the diverse and hostile races in the Near East, the League of Nations was specified as the organization to deal with the difficulty. All through this document—the latest great international contract that has been drafted—we find the idea constantly present that the League of Nations is the natural authority to which to appeal when unquestioned impartiality and wisdom are demanded.

Here is another instance that I cannot discuss here except with great discretion. Very recently, as the result of an international difference of an exceedingly acute and complex character of which we have all heard through the press, the feebler of the parties appealed to the League to settle a dispute that had arisen between it and its neighbor. The mere fact that the controversy between Italy and Greece was submitted to the League is of itself testimony to the impartiality, the probity, and the courage of that body. I am most hopeful for the future.

Some people think it is imprudent to bestow too many tasks upon the League; they fear it will be crushed by its burdens. That is not my opinion. I believe that it will be far less endangered by having an excess of duties thrust upon it than by being disregarded where great international problems are at stake, and left to deal merely with matters of minor importance. That would be a disaster. The real danger does not lie in overstrain, but in idleness, routine, and apathy; for this is not an ordinary machine.

Indeed, the League is not a machine at all, it is a living organism, a body that obeys the universal laws of life. It must either grow or diminish. If it abandons itself to indolence and inertia, if it is allowed to become flabby and weak in idleness, it will lose its strength. But if, on the other hand, every function is kept employed and active, it will continue to grow and develop like any other living organism, and attain its maximum force and power. For my part, I do not believe that the League can be killed by too much activity. It is created to grow. Its functions compel that. But in what direction, and to what extent is that growth possible? Nothing is more dangerous than prophecy. We have an English saying never to prophesy what we do not know, which is equivalent to saying that we should never prophesy. However, I may venture to say one thing—by studying the past of a living organism you can foresee to some extent its future. The League of Nations is four years old. We can at least review what it has done up to the present.

The League Today

It will be illuminating, in taking you back, to compare what the League of Nations is to-day with what it was in 1920. I have a very lively recollection of that. I recall that when I came to the first Assembly, in 1920, doubt and hesitation weighed upon us—upon myself and those who were better qualified than I to judge what the future might bring forth. The general opinion was that the first

---

Preamble to the Covenant of the League of Nations—1919

The High Contracting Parties,

In order to promote international cooperation and to achieve international peace and security
by the acceptance of obligations not to resort to war,
by the prescription of open, just and honorable relations between nations,
by the firm establishment of the understandings of international law as the actual rule of conduct among Governments,
and by the maintenance of justice and a scrupulous respect for all treaty obligations in the dealings of organised peoples with one another,

Agree to this Covenant of the League of Nations.

Assembly of the League would speedily prove it to be a naive and utopian conception. It was predicted that when so many different nations met together they would immediately set to quarreling with each other, and wreck the whole organization. I see before me my friend, M. Hymans, who performed such good service as the President of that first Assembly. He will remember the howls of triumph from the enemies of the League when a South American Government withdrew from the Assembly. That Government, I am happy to say, is now proposing to come back. It has already taken a definite and very helpful step in that direction by paying up its past contributions to the League....

All the unfavorable prognostications that greeted us have been disproved. Our difficulties have been surmounted, and to-day we see the nations of the world working together. We now know that by bringing together under one roof the delegates of the most distant countries, of the most diverse religions and races, of the most alien civilizations, and by working fifteen days together, as we did in the first Assembly, we speedily banish our sense of differences, we become a united body, acting as if all our members had identical antecedents and traditions.

I shall not describe further this first Assembly. I merely ask you to consider, now, the present Assembly, which opens next Monday. There will be fifty-two States represented, and two more applying for admission. You will see not only former Allies working shoulder to shoulder with former neutrals, but you will also see several former enemy Governments taking their part in the common labor for peace. Everyone is agreed that, as soon as circumstances permit, the circle of the League of Nations will enlarge until it embraces all the world....

League Activities

Permit me to enumerate briefly the principal organized activities of the League. They are the Commissions on Finance, Economics, Sanitation, Opium, White Slavery, and Labor. Then there are several missions dealing with refugees, the administration of the Saar and of Danzig, and the High Commission for Austria. Furthermore, there are the various conferences that have been held, such as the Financial Conference at Brussels, the Communications Conference at Barcelona, and the White Slave Conference, without including the Labor Conferences and all the good service they have rendered. In addition, there is the service of the League in repatriating war prisoners, which is closely associated with the refugee problem, and the reconstruction of Austria. All these things, and many others that I might mention, are being practically carried out on a basis of international cooperation through the League of Nations, and are more or less directly associated with its principal object, which is to restore peace in the world....

I foresee a time when every great international conflict will be submitted to the League of Nations as naturally as disputes between individuals are submitted to courts of law. It will eventually seem just as impossible and absurd for a nation to make war as it would be for an individual in a modern State to try to settle his title to property by violence. That is the great goal I see before us....

We must prevent the Hercules of prejudice, of militarism, of bureaucracy, of apathy, from separating the League of Nations from the peoples of the world from whom it draws its strength. If we maintain that contact, if we draw into the movement the common people of the whole world, you may be assured that we have nothing to fear from our enemies. We shall advance surely and rapidly toward the achievement of our grand ideal, toward the time

31

when force and violence will no longer rule the world, when an attempt to crush a little nation, to exaggerate a national claim, to disregard justice, will be as rare, indeed rarer among nations than it is to-day among civilized individuals. That is our goal. It is a great goal; no greater could be set before the peoples of the world.

Let us not falter in our duty. We are facing the most glorious opportunity that has ever been set before mankind. How shall we justify ourselves to our children and our children's children if, through our apathy, our indolence, our lack of energy, we fail to carry forward to triumph this great effort for the welfare of humanity?

"*The League, as now framed and operated, is incapable of bringing about moral reconciliation between peoples.*"

The League Is Not Working

J.L. Garvin

J.L. Garvin was perhaps the most prolific and widely read journalist of his day in Great Britain. A political liberal, he was editor of the *Observer*, a Sunday paper published in London. In the following viewpoint, Mr. Garvin explains why he believes that the League of Nations cannot work as presently constituted.

As you read, consider the following:

1. According to the author, what two necessities must be met in order for the League to succeed as savior of the world?
2. What is the author's concern regarding Germany? Russia? the United States?
3. According to the author, which countries dominate the Executive Council of the League?

J.L. Garvin, "A Shattered Peace Pillar," *Living Age*, December 15, 1923. Published originally in *The Observer*, October 14, 1923. Reprinted with the permission of *The Observer*, London.

Those who most believe in the original purpose and plan of the League are the most bound to recognize that as at present constituted and worked it does not begin to fulfill either its spiritual or its practical functions and never can be capable of the offices for which it was created....

Needless to say that the League as it exists has done a vast amount of excellent work on side-issues and subordinate questions. But we must look to the main thing. We must acknowledge that the League, as now framed and operated, is incapable of bringing about moral reconciliation between peoples; of replacing the reign of force by a reign of law impartially applied; of arresting the appalling regrowth of armaments; and of saving the general peace. In a word the League as we see it is not strong enough for any of its purposes, and has not even had the courage of its weakness.

Profound Moral Defect

What are the reasons for these things? The first truth to face is that the League as it stands is founded upon a spiritual evasion of its greatest original purpose. It has persisted in that evasion for four years, and until the profound moral defect is mended the chaos of practical evils never can be remedied. The letter of the Covenant has miscarried right and left, because the spirit that gives life has never resided in the existing body. Let us go back for a moment to the origins. In past history wars had still led to more wars. Nearly every great treaty of peace, expressing nothing more than the temporary domination and egotistical will of the victors, had sown the seeds of new conflicts, as in the terrible but deep fable of the Dragon's Teeth. It was plain in the midst of Armageddon that on these terms white civilization would perish, and that its science would only ensure its suicide.

Men of competent thought had to seek a new way of salvation for the world. For this, two things above all were imperative. The first necessity was to curb the traditional acquisitiveness of conquest and to make a moderate peace, with a view to the reconciliation of the belligerents. The second necessity was to create, as the permanent organ of that reconciliation, a true and general League of Nations. Such a League, to be worthy of its name or equal to its purposes, would have to include victors, vanquished, and neutrals alike. For the supreme aim of world-peace no lower or narrower spirit would serve.

But when the League was founded, it became in fact, and has remained, the instrument of the Allies and their clients. Germany was excluded by what we have ventured to call the supreme spiritual evasion of all history. Russia was excluded, although without the immeasurable sacrifices of the Russian people through three years not even the whole power of the United States could have enabled the Allies to win the war. Until these omissions are repaired, the fatal weakness of the League for its moral and practical functions alike will continue to lurk in the very root of it, and will vitiate its being more and more.

When America went out of the peace there was a worse situation. With Germany and Russia still excluded after the United States had withdrawn, the League of Nations lost all true title to that great name. It ceased to represent an effective majority of the white race. It ceased above all to be a valid authority in Europe taken as a whole; and Europe must be taken as a whole if there is to be any chance for world-peace. Nominally the yellow, brown, and black races are fully represented at Geneva, though the huge majority of their innumerable millions have never heard of it. By contrast white civilization is left a broken thing, half in the League, half out of it. Political mockery never imagined a satire more scathing than this reality. The League's main work is to restore as far as possible the solidarity of white civilization, and while this is neglected, and until this is thoroughly attempted, so far at least as Europe is concerned, everything else will be in vain. The fundamental work cannot be done; it cannot even be attempted. After America went out it was sheer life and death for the hopes of the League to bring in Germany and Russia.

Forces of Destruction

The world cannot tolerate forever a system which allows force, past or present, to decide the ownership of materials which are the foundation of our daily life. While it hesitates to face this problem of economic imperialism, the League is tolerating the growth of the forces and motives which one day will destroy it, and civilization with it.

Henry N. Brailsford, *The Nation*, February 2, 1927.

Germany and Russia together represent two hundred millions of white people. While these are excluded the composition of the League is a fantastic travesty of its original intention and right purpose. Fifty-four nations are represented at Geneva. They include miscroscopic Luxemburg and minute Panama. They include Haiti and Liberia; Honduras and Nicaragua; Costa Rica and San Salvador. Abyssinia is the latest recruit to be solemnly enrolled. We desire to speak with respect of all these signatories of the Covenant. Yet of the fifty-four nations now included we could name twenty whose inhabitants put together would number no more than half the population of Germany. Out of the whole of these fifty-four nations we could name nearly forty whose total population does not exceed that of Russia alone. But while Haiti is in the League and the German people out of it; while chaotic China is included but recovering Russia not, it is idle to say that the fundamental conceptions of political justice and sanity, or even the rudiments of working common-sense, are yet properly represented at Geneva. While this state of things remains, an element of obvious mockery will mar the name of the League; there will be a flaw in its title; the effective weight of civilization will not be behind it; nor can it begin to be capable in practice of applying the principles which the Covenant declares.

Is It Working?

So much for the composition of the League. What of its working? The League is dominated in fact by the Executive Council. That Council in turn is dominated by four Great Powers only—Britain, France, Italy, and Japan. At the best it is an instrument of the chief European victors. At the best it bears no resemblance to that impartial reconciling governing body which every real advocate of the League during the war desired to create and declared to be necessary. At the best the life and the truth by which the League was meant to be informed cannot reside in such a close corporation. But in reality the control is yet narrower than this analysis has yet suggested. Japan does not care to meddle too much with the affairs of Europe. Italy in the present phase has other reasons for reserve. France and Britain are left as the sole forces which can actuate the League. But France is concentrated on her own concerns, and the whole spirit of her policy today derives straight from Richelieu and Napoleon. It is the spirit, not of the Covenant, but of the older diplomacy, backed by arms and alliances.

It comes to this. Whenever Britain and France agree much can be done. When they differ nothing can be done. France, at will, can stop or start the machinery of the League; and she will not allow the principles of the Covenant to be impartially applied whenever her own proceedings or those of her clients are seriously involved. Though nominally representing fifty-four nations, Geneva is in the custody of the Quai d'Orsay; and M. Poincaré beyond all question is the paramount force in Europe. From this state of things the Vilna, Ruhr, and Corfu crises have successively resulted. They have done more harm than the Covenant has yet done good. Until Russia and Germany are included so as to establish something like a real working majority in Europe—until the basis of the Assembly is broadened and the character of its Council correspondingly changed—the League of Nations cannot begin to be what was intended, a steady, effectual, impartial power, acting up to the great spirit of the Covenant, and applying the letter of its principles as an equal law for all alike.

*

"Foremost in importance among the devices primarily for the preservation of peace is the League of Nations."

For the League of Nations

Clarence K. Streit

Clarence K. Streit was a newspaper columnist and author who spent much of his professional career as an advocate of world government. He graduated from Montana State University and attended Oxford University in 1920 and 1921 on a Rhodes Scholarship. From 1925 to 1939 he was *The New York Times'* League of Nations and Washington Bureau correspondent. His books include *Freedom Against Itself* and *The New Federalist.* In the following viewpoint, Mr. Streit attacks critics of the League. He argues that given time and faith, the League of Nations can become the most important agency of international conciliation in the world.

As you read, consider the following questions:

1. Why does the author compare the League of Nations to a flying machine?
2. How does Mr. Streit respond to criticisms of the League?

Clarence K. Streit, "The World's Efforts to Attain Peace," *The New York Times Magazine,* August 12, 1934. © 1934 by The New York Times Company. Reprinted by permission.

There was no League of Nations on this day twenty years ago, when Germany was completing the subjugation of Belgium and preparing to invade France in force. Men had dreamed for thousands of years of stopping war, just as they had dreamed of flying. By 1914, they had discovered a way to fly, though the machinery was crude, dangerous. Often it killed. But sometimes it worked. There was not even crude machinery in 1914 for preventing war.

There were, it is true, these time-tried methods: armaments and Ambassadors, secret arming and secret diplomacy. But these were designed not to make peace but to win wars, to keep not peace but truces so long as they were advantageous.

There were some arbitration treaties, but they carefully reserved to the ordeal of war the settlement of all disputes involving "national honor" or "vital interests." There had been speeches from time to time in favor of a World Court. A peace congress had met at The Hague in 1907, but nothing had been done in seven years to remedy its failure.

No government was under any obligation to try to settle without bloodshed any serious dispute, or even to consult face to face with other governments. Indeed, as Sir Edward Grey found to his and mankind's grief, merely to seek to improvise at the last hour a conference to prevent war was worse than vain.

No one knew in 1914 that war in four years could kill 13,000,000 men all round the world. War then was not the most abominable of crimes. It was no crime at all. It was the field of honor. There was everything designed to make war. There was nothing designed to prevent it.

The World Since the League

Now, twenty years after, neither this nor its reverse is true. There is still danger of war. There is still everything to make war. But now there are some things to prevent it, some things designed solely to keep peace—not things like War Offices and Foreign Offices, for which "peace" is sometimes a by-product. The new peace machinery is as crude, measured by the job it is designed to do, as was the flying machinery of twenty years ago. It has not yet gone round the world. It has not always worked. But it has worked sometimes.

First in time and foremost in importance among the devices primarily for the preservation of peace is the League of Nations. It seeks to do its work through the organs it has created and the obligations its members have accepted. Its aim is to prevent all international conflicts, including those involving national honor, vital interests and treaty revision. It seeks continuous cooperation before conflict comes for the peaceful settlement of disputes, once they arise, by conciliation, private consultation, public conference, judicial decision, arbitration; and for the maintenance by force—

moral, economic or military—of a system of law against those who refuse to respect it otherwise.

The League organs—Assembly, Council, Secretariat, International Labor Organization, Permanent Court for International Justice, economic, financial, transit, health, information and education sections—are numerous, permanent, with a proved capacity for growth. The League obligations, though leaving some loopholes for war, are comprehensive.

The League covenant no longer stands alone. There is a peace pact by which some sixty governments declare war a crime, renounce it as an instrument of national policy and pledge themselves to settle all disputes peacefully. The pact is more drastic in its undertaking than the covenant, but it has no machinery for its execution. It depends for execution on the circumstance that all the important States that are bound to use the covenant's execution machinery have bound themselves also to the pact's objectives, and two more States besides, the United States and Soviet Russia.

Nor is this all the peace machinery that has developed in the past twenty years. There are the Washington treaties—Naval, Nine-Power, Four-Power—the Locarno treaty, the London naval treaty, the optional clause by which twoscore governments have opted for the compulsory jurisdiction of the World Court, the general act by which a score of them have tightened the obligatory character of conciliation or arbitration for disputes among them. There are hundreds of bilateral treaties for conciliation, arbitration, judicial settlement, non-aggression.

Civilized Nations Should Combine

The one effective move for obtaining peace is by an agreement among all the great powers in which each should pledge itself not only to abide by the decisions of a common tribunal but to back its decisions by force. The great civilized nations should combine by solemn agreement in a great world league for the peace of righteousness.

Theodore Roosevelt.

The peace machinery that has developed since 1914 is far more comprehensive than many realize. Since it began with the adoption of the covenant there have been more threats of war, if anything, than ever before—for a great fire leaves many sparks. But since then not one big war has been declared. There has been fighting, but the hostilities have been minor affairs compared even with the Balkan Wars, the Russo-Japanese War and the Spanish-American War—the kind of thing that was breaking out somewhere in the world every five or ten years before the League began functioning.

Yet there is now widespread through the world a feeling of disillusionment often bordering on despair regarding the League and all this peace machinery.

Certainly the League has not measured up to the great hopes entertained for such an organization in the days of the "war to end war," the "war to make the world safe for democracy." It apparently seems to many in retrospect that the whole war was fought solely and consciously to create the League. One gets the impression from the way people now voice their disappointment in the League—the bitter-enders then being naturally most bitterly disillusioned now—that it was the League which filled the front page during the war and during the peace conference, and that everything since then had centered on perfecting the peace machinery.

The disillusionment, in fact, seems to be at least partly due to a curiously widespread illusion. It seems to have been completely forgotten that the League of Nations was so much the poor relation of the peace conference that the commission which drafted the covenant had to sit mostly after office hours. President Wilson alone among the great-power leaders attended its meetings; such statesmen as Lloyd George and Clemenceau did not have time to bother with making machinery for preventing the slaughter of another 13,000,000 men....

Criticism of the League

It was not generally expected of the Wright brothers that they prove the value of their flying machine by flying around the world or even across the Atlantic the first time they left the ground. The marvel was that they could stay in the air at all. But did people marvel when the new peace machinery actually stopped war between Greece and Bulgaria? Or did they belittle this achievement and the peaceful settlement of the Mosul question, the Austro-German customs protocol, the Anglo-Persian oil dispute, the hostilities between Peru and Colombia?

Do or do not people now condemn the League as a hopeless failure because it has not kept a great military power out of Manchuria; because it has not already remedied all the mistakes made at Versailles; because it has not cured the world's economic, monetary and armament ills at the first world conferences ever assembled to cure them? It is generally held that its failures have, after all, cost relatively few lives and given invaluable lessons for strengthening its machinery. Or is the notion widespread that because of its failures and because its writ cannot yet be trusted to run around the world the League should be thrown on the ash-heap; that men should stick entirely to the old-fashioned ways of secret armaments and secret diplomacy?

If one asks, whether in France, England or America, the reason for disappointment in the League, for belief in the dismal failure of the peace machinery, the answer usually is that the Disarma-

THE LEAGUE OF NATIONS ARGUMENT IN A NUTSHELL.

ment Conference has not yet brought security (say the French) or disarmament (say the English and Americans). And all answer that the League and the peace pact and the Nine-Power treaty failed to meet the Japanese test. The conclusion is drawn that all this peace machinery put together cannot be trusted to prevent that "next great war" which is forever alarming the war-shocked generation of 1914-18.

If one questions further, all the complaints of people against the League and other peace machinery seem everywhere to boil down to this: the League is too weak, too slow, too cumbersome. People talk of it exactly as they talked of Congress under the Articles of Confederation: "It can declare anything, but it can do nothing."

This criticism seems especially to prevail among Americans. There was a time when many people everywhere feared the League would be too powerful. That was precisely why the drafters of its convenant saddled it with such devices as the unanimity rule, whereby any single sovereign State can legally block action. They were more concerned at the start with the brakes than with the motor.

The League Must Be Given a Chance

There was a time when, despite the fifty-nation-power brakes on a one-nation-power motor, Americans refused to go into Wilson's League or lend it any of their strength because they thought it was too strong, a "super-State." There was a time—merely six years ago—when irreconcilable American Senators consented to the peace pact only because they considered it "a pious wish." Now it seems Americans in one breath condemn the League as being hopelessly supine and in the next breath refuse to strengthen it by supplying the missing part which American entry alone can supply—for, after all, this League mechanism was designed by an American to function with the United States as one of its essential cogs.

The question seems to be whether the old fear that the League is too strong will kill it or whether the new fear that it is too weak will cause it to be made stronger.

If the despondent character of the talk of the day is the only clue to the future of the League, then the outlook is black. But if the development of machinery in the realm of transportation gives any indication, it is not so dark. People held mass meetings against that devilish contrivance of Stephenson's that hurtled man along at the "frightful" speed of fifteen miles an hour. But people did not go back to the stage-coach. They went on to the airplane.

Political machinery, of course, may evolve differently. So far, however, its evolution seems to have followed the same general line. The American Union certainly was not born full-fledged. It first grew through the Confederation. The Articles of Confederation gave Congress hardly more power than the covenant gives the League. Yet it took years to get the thirteen States to ratify these articles, even while they were fighting together against England, because people thought the articles created a super-State dangerous to their individual freedom.

But when experience proved that the articles were too weak, when the thirteen sovereign States fell a prey to worse and worse economic, financial and social ills culminating in Shay's Rebellion, when people began to believe that the danger to their freedom lay in the weakness of this American league, they did not scrap the Confederation and turn backward. They went on and made so strong a Union that their own only war among themselves thereafter was to prove that it could keep its members from seceding from it.

The "failure" of the League may result otherwise, but only if history does not repeat itself.

"Since it is extremely difficult for the League to reform itself, as far as we are concerned it can perish in peace."

Against the League of Nations

Benito Mussolini

Between 1934 and 1936, Italy engaged in a series of military operations aimed at conquering and annexing Ethiopia. Italy's actions were in direct violation of Article 10 of the Covenant of the League of Nations, which insured the preservation of the territorial integrity of all member states. A series of sanctions directed toward Italy ultimately proved fruitless. Realizing that the League was not taking any effective action, the government of Italy hastened to "officially" annex Ethiopia. On May 9, 1936, the King of Italy decreed that "the territories and peoples which belonged to the Empire of Ethiopia are placed under the full and entire sovereignty of the Kingdom of Italy. The title of Emperor of Ethiopia is assumed by the King of Italy for himslef and his successors." The following viewpoint is taken from a speech Benito Mussolini, fascist dictator of Italy, delivered before a gathering of his followers in Milan on November 2, 1936. In it, he consigns the League of Nations to the graveyard of history.

As you read, consider the following questions:

1. What examples did Mussolini cite in referring to the illusions of Wilsonian ideology?
2. How did Mussolini suggest that the Italian people "make a policy of peace"?

Blackshirts of Milan: By means of the speech which I am about to make to you and for which I ask, and you will give me, a few dozen minutes of your attention, I intend to lay down the position of Fascist Italy with regard to its relations with other peoples in this so turgid and disquieting moment.

The high level of your political education allows me to lay before you those problems which elsewhere are debated in so-called Parliaments, even at so-called democratic banquets.

I shall be extremely brief, but I add that every one of my words has been weighed.

If one wishes to clarify the European atmosphere it is first necessary to clear the table of all illusions, of all conventional falsehoods and the lies that still constitute relics of the great shipwreck of Wilsonian ideology.

One of these illusions is already flat, the illusion of disarmament. No one wishes to disarm first, and for all to disarm together is impossible and absurd....

The Absurdity of the League

For us Fascisti, in the habit of examining with cool eye the reality of life in history, another illusion we reject is that which passed by the name of collective security. Collective security never existed, does not exist, and will never exist. A virile people provides within its borders its collective security and refuses to confide its destiny to uncertain hands of third persons.

Another illusion it is necessary to reject is indivisible peace. Indivisible peace could have only this meaning, indivisible war. Thus, peoples refuse, and justly so, to fight for interests that do not concern them.

The League of Nations is based on the absurdity of the principle of absolute juridical parity among all States; whereas the States are different from one another, at least from the viewpoint of their historic responsibility.

For the League of Nations the dilemma is expressed in very clear terms, either to reform itself or to perish. Since it is extremely difficult for the League to reform itself, as far as we are concerned it can perish in peace.

At any event, we have not forgotten and we will not forget that the League of Nations has organized by methods of diabolical diligence an iniquitous siege against the people of Italy and tried to starve her men, women and children, tried to shatter our military force and the work of civilization being carried on 2,500 to 5,000 miles distant in another land.

It did not succeed, not because it did not want to, but because it found itself faced by the compact unity of the Italian people, capable of all sacrifices and also of fighting the fifty-two coalition States.

Now, in order to make a policy of peace it is not necessary to pass through the corridors of the League of Nations....

Milan comrades, let us turn to our own affairs: Marching orders for the fifth year of fascism are the following:

Peace with all, with those near and afar. Armed peace! Therefore, our program of armaments for land, sea and sky will be regularly developed.

The Nobility of War

War alone brings up to its highest tension all human energy, and puts the stamp of nobility upon the peoples who have the courage to meet it. All other trials are substitutes, which never really put men into the position where they have to make the great decision—the alternatives of life or death.

Benito Mussolini, 1935.

Acceleration of all productive energies of the nation, in agricultural and industrial fields. Development of the corporative system to its definite realization.

But here is a duty I confide to you, oh Milanese of this most ardent and most Fascist Milan which has revealed its great soul these days. I confide in you, oh Milanese of this generous working and untiring Milan, this duty:

You must place yourselves, as you will place yourselves, as an advance guard for the development of the empire so as to make it in the shortest possible period an element of well-being, of power of glory for the nation.

Understanding Words in Context

Readers occasionally come across words which they do not recognize. And frequently, because they do not know a word or words, they will not fully understand the passage being read. Obviously, the reader can look up an unfamiliar word in a dictionary. However, by carefully examining the word in the context in which it is used, the word's meaning can often be determined. A careful reader may find clues to the meaning of the word in surrounding words, ideas, and attitudes.

Below are excerpts from the viewpoints in this chapter. In each excerpt, one or two words are printed in italics. Try to determine the meaning of each word by reading the excerpt. Under each excerpt you will find four definitions for the italicized word. Choose the one that is closest to your understanding of the word.

Finally, use a dictionary to see how well you have understood the words in context. It will be helpful to discuss with others the clues which helped you decide on each word's meaning.

1. Unless you get the united, *CONCERTED* purpose and power of the great Governments of the world behind this settlement, it will fall down like a house of cards.

   CONCERTED means:
   a) agreed on   c) uneasy
   b) concentrated   d) melodic

2. It has been *REITERATED* here on this floor, and reiterated to the point of weariness, that in every treaty there is some sacrifice of sovereignty.

   REITERATED means:
   a) scheduled   c) assumed
   b) repeated   d) reissued

3. We would not have our country's vigor exhausted, or her moral force *ABATED*, by everlasting meddling in every quarrel which afflicts the world.

   ABATED means:
   a) omitted
   b) reconsidered
   c) put on
   d) reduced

4. The mere fact that the controversy between Italy and Greece was submitted to the League is of itself testimony to the impartiality, the *PROBITY*, and the courage of that body.

   PROBITY means:
   a) ineffectiveness
   b) color
   c) probability
   d) honesty

5. All the unfavorable *PROGNOSTICATIONS* that were made have been disproved.

   PROGNOSTICATIONS means:
   a) predictions
   b) prescriptions
   c) practical matters
   d) wishes

6. Wholly on the positive side, people of good will everywhere, and they are *LEGION*, want to share the good things of life both materially and spiritually.

   LEGION means:
   a) angry
   b) numerous
   c) armed
   d) expectant

7. By recognizing the League as a dangerous weapon, you will be better able to see its *PERNICIOUS* effects.

   PERNICIOUS means:
   a) destructive
   b) picky
   c) powerful
   d) disgusting

8. Until these omissions are repaired, the fatal moral weakness of the League will continue to lurk in the very root of it, and will *VITIATE* its being more and more.

   VITIATE means:
   a) inspire
   b) raise
   c) degrade
   d) create

9. Instead of being an effective instrument for conflict resolution, the League serves all too often as an arena in which conflict is extended and *EXACERBATED*.

   EXACERBATED means:
   a) tried again
   b) reduced
   c) broken down
   d) made worse

Bibliography

The following list of books, periodicals, and pamphlets deals with the subject matter of this chapter.

B.D. Allinson
"Life or Death for the League," *The Nation*, November 4, 1925.

Donald S. Birn
The League of Nations. New York: Oxford University Press, 1981.

H.N. Braelsford
"League of Nations: A Misprint in History," *The Nation*, February 2, 1927.

Harriet E. Davis
Pioneers in World Order. Salem, NH: Ayer Co., 1944.

H. Feis
"Successful League of Nations: The Basis of European Security," *Annals of the American Academy of Political and Social Science*, July 1926.

Raymond B. Fosdick
Letters on the League of Nations. Princeton, NJ: Princeton University Press, 1966.

W. Irwin
"Did the League of Nations Fail?" *Colliers*, November 3, 1923.

L.P. Jacks
"League of Nations or a League of Governments?" *Atlantic Monthly*, February 1923.

James A. Joyce
Broken Star: The Story of the League of Nations, 1919-39. Atlantic Highlands, NJ: Humanities Press, 1978.

Literary Digest
"Living Argument for the League," April 14, 1923.

Sally Marks
The Illusion of Peace: International Relations 1918-1933. New York: St. Martin's Press, 1976.

Francis S. Marvin
Evolution of World-Peace: Essays. Salem, NH: Ayer Co., 1921.

S. Rice
"Problems of the League," *Fortune*, May 1924.

Ralph A. Stone
Wilson and the League of Nations: Why America's Rejection? Melbourne, FL: Krieger Publishing, 1978.

United Nations

Internationalism

Introduction

During World War II, the idea of an international organization to insure peace, one that would replace the moribund League of Nations, gestated in the minds of Roosevelt, Churchill and other leaders of the world's great powers. When the war was over, the fifty-one nations that had been allied against Germany and Japan met in San Francisco to establish the United Nations and sign its charter. It was hoped that this organization would keep peace where the League had failed.

The United Nations is structured around a General Assembly and a Security Council. All member nations are admitted to the General Assembly where each has one vote, but only fifteen nations at a time sit on the Security Council. Five of these—the United States, the Soviet Union, Great Britain, France and China—are permanent and hold veto power within the council. The other ten council members rotate on two-year terms.

In many respects, the UN has proved more effective than the League of Nations whose weak attempts at maintaining peace through sanctions and forums were largely ignored. Part of the UN's success has come from the peacekeeping military forces which it has employed in areas such as Cyprus, the Sinai Peninsula, and the buffer zone between North and South Korea. In these cases, the presence of the multinational UN force has served to pacify the areas, thus averting the eruption of a wider conflict. On the other hand, it was unable to keep peace during other crises such as the Vietnam War, the Arab-Israeli Wars of 1967 and 1973, and the India-Pakistan War of 1971. In most of these and similar incidents it failed either because one of the five permanent Security Council members vetoed UN intervention or because warring nations ignored its actions.

John Trever, *The Albuquerque Journal*, reprinted with permission.

Although the ultimate success or failure of the United Nations remains to be decided, its efficacy and worthiness has been the subject of national and international debate since its inception. This chapter highlights those issues most frequently cited both in support of and in opposition to the UN. The viewpoints are taken from a broad range of sources and represent, among others, the opinions of academicians, journalists, and an internationally respected former secretary-general of the UN.

"The United Nations appears to be the best mechanism yet devised for bringing into harmony the conflicting desires of nations."

The United Nations Promotes Harmony

Russell D. Brackett

Russell D. Brackett has written extensively in the areas of international affairs and intercultural education. An educator and author, he is a Minnesota resident who served as a board member of the Minnesota World Affairs Center and the Minnesota United Nations Association. He has also served as a member of the Advisory Committee of the United World Federalists. In the following viewpoint, Mr. Brackett lists six reasons why he believes that the United Nations should be an integral part of today's world.

As you read, consider the following questions:

1. Why does the author claim that the United Nations is "a sheer necessity"?
2. How does the author relate American aid to the United Nations?

Russell D. Brackett, *Pathways to Peace*, Minneapolis: T.S. Denison & Company, 1965. Reprinted by permission.

The world of the mid-twentieth century bears small resemblance to the same world a hundred or even fifty years earlier. Change, often coming with annoying swiftness, is perhaps the only certainty of this space age. The inevitability of change makes each new decade different from the preceding one.

The fundamental changes that focus the attention of the world's millions on the need for a working instrument of law and order at the international level are several. Among the more obvious changes are the following:

1. The once formidable protection offered a lucky few nations by wide bodies of water and rugged mountain ranges exists no more. Man's ability to make faster than sound flight over celestial thoroughfares has obliterated the former effectiveness of massive physical barriers. No physical environmental mass anywhere today provides man natural protection. An international U.N. police force might be the best substitute.

2. Increasingly the people of the world are realizing the depth and extent of man's interdependence economically, socially and geographically. The availability of mass air communication in the mid-twentieth century accentuates this interdependence. The United Nations is but the political manifestation of this closely knit world.

Just as no man lives alone, so no nation can live unto itself. Albert Einstein said, "Today no man is an island: Our fate is linked with that of our fellow man throughout the world."

A Rapidly Changing World

3. The unbelievably rapid, almost fantastic development of air transportation, stimulated by global wars and man's desire to explore space, has surely knit the world together in one communication fabric as it has never been tied before. A. T. & T.'s Telestar added a new dimension in 1964 to the world of communication.

Alan Shepard in May 1961, climbed into his Mercury capsule atop a fuming Redstone Missile. In his fifteen-minute space ride, Shepard set the tone of travel for the new decade. In years ahead, space will all but surrender to man's ingenuity. The earth, mysterious and unknown to eighteenth-century explorers sailing for months to reach an unknown destination, today seems so small. Jules Verne's novel *Around the World in Eighty Days*, was long ago old-fashioned and as out of date as Henry Ford's Model T. Time will have new meaning when observing manned satellites circling the world every hour or two becomes a nightly occurrence....

The UN in Today's World

This ever-changing world demands new kinds of controls. The U.N. must stand by.

4. The age of nuclear weapons with its ugly portent of massive

death and destruction on a scale yet undreamed of, focuses man's attention on his need for international agreement, controlling disarmament under a stronger United Nations.

In a world of sovereign powers armed with weapons of total destruction, the world's people, in a Churchillian phrase, are "roaming and peering around on the rim of hell."

International organization control of armaments is clearly indicated. Does any international organization exist except the U.N.

PEACE FLAG OR BATTLE FLAGS?

Justus in the *Minneapolis Star.* Reprinted by permission.

under whose surveillance this might be accomplished? The United Nations becomes a sheer necessity.

5. Not only is nuclear war unthinkable, but the burden of today's arms cost is intolerably heavy. No sacrifice, for sure, is too great to protect the national interest under any conditions if there are no alternatives. But dreamy realists in every nation are hoping for the day when but a fraction of the fifty billion currently spent for defense can be diverted preferably through the U.N. to constructive, not destructive, uses. Improving health, raising educational

---

Last Hope for Peace

The peoples of the earth turn to the United Nations as the last hope of concord and peace; we presume to present here, with their tribute of honor and of hope, our own tribute also....

The edifice which you have constructed must never fall; it must be perfected and made equal to the needs which world history will permit.

Pope Paul, address before UN General Assembly, October 4, 1965.

---

levels, relieving areas of poverty, all problems plaguing over half the world's population, should be the U.N.'s top priority of business, granted the necessary financial resources. These resources might more easily be available were freedom granted from the currently excessive burden of defense spending. An effective limitation and reduction of national armaments would open the door to the solution of these depressing global humanitarian problems. Only the U.N. is available to help open this door....

The UN and the Common Good

6. Wholly on the positive side and for compelling reasons, men of good will everywhere, and they are legion, want to share the good things of life both materially and spiritually. Except through international organization how can the principle of the "common good" be applied to international society?

Former President Eisenhower put it this way: *"Every bomb we can manufacture, every plane, every ship, every gun, in the long run has no purpose other than negative—to give us time to prevent the other fellow from starting a war, since we know we won't. The billions we pour into munitions ought to be supported by a great American effort, a positive constructive effort that leads directly toward what we all want: a true and lasting peace."*

Working through the U.N., American aid hopefully might support an integrated international attack on the world's major ills. What higher motive than peace can be mustered in defense of the U.N.?

On April 10, 1963, Pope John, speaking to Catholics and non-Catholics alike, indicated he hoped the United Nations eventually might become a strong world authority. The Pope said it was his "earnest wish" that the United Nations be given structure and means to safeguard peace. A supra-national authority must be considered, the Pope added, because national leaders in the modern world are "on a footing of equality" and are "no longer capable of facing the task of finding an adequate solution to the problems."

In summary, the United Nations appears to be the best mechanism yet devised for bringing into harmony the conflicting desires of nations in order to maintain peace and security.

"The United Nations is working but it is not working for advancing the purposes of the Charter."

The United Nations Promotes Conflict

Abraham Yeselson

Abraham Yeselson has researched extensively the role the United Nations plays in maintaining international peace and security. A professor of political science at Rutgers University, he is a specialist in foreign relations and has conducted numerous international seminars abroad. The following viewpoint is edited from testimony delivered by the author at a hearing of the Senate Committee on Foreign Relations. In it, Dr. Yeselson argues that the United Nations tends to operate in almost constant violation of its Charter.

As you read, consider the following questions:

1. What, in the author's opinion, is the correct way to evaluate the United Nations?
2. How does the author suggest that American officers respond to the practices of the United Nations?

From testimony delivered by Dr. Abraham Yeselson before the Senate Committee on Foreign Relations on May 8, 1975.

Over a long period of time I began to question the knowledge which had been imparted to me and the theories upon which they were based and I came out in a very funny place in a very uncomfortable place. I came out in a place which says in effect that the proper approach to the United Nations is not from the aspect of the ideals of the Charter or the principles of the organization, but that in order to understand what happens there and how the organization is used, and especially its impact on conflict, it's necessary to approach the organization from the point of view of the motivation of those who use the organization. It took me, perhaps because I am slow, some 15 years to ask a new question. The new question was, "who brings what issues to the United Nations and why?"

And from that perspective those explanations for what happened at the United Nations acquired a completely different meaning. I understood things better and I believe that I now have the basis for really analyzing how the United Nations contributes to conflict.

From this point of view I answer your fundamental question by saying, yes, the United Nations is working but it is not working for advancing the purposes of the Charter, the principles of the organization, and it is not working in the interests of American foreign policy.

National Issues Dominate the UN

I am not going to be presumptuous and try to advise you on what American foreign policy should be; but if we view the United Nations, we see clearly that it is now an instrument for the advancement of the foreign policy of those who can dominate it....

In every instance, using various strategies which I cannot detail here, states advance national interests, introducing an issue into the United Nations is always for the achievement of a conflict purpose. The effect is always to embitter relations among the States and the impact on the conflict as a result of the introduction of this weapon is to widen the conflict and make it more difficult to solve peacefully and less likely that the dispute will be resolved.

Misuse of the UN Charter

From my peculair point of view I find, for example, that the Middle East conflict is in large part a result of the United Nations' intervention, and that if peace will be achieved there it will be achieved in spite of the United Nations.

The same is true in respect to the Koreans. After 25 years of resolutions at the United Nations, essentially in support of South Korea, if and when any normalization of relations will be achieved in the Koreas, it will be accomplished in spite of what has happened at the United Nations and not because of what has happened....It is nationalism and sovereignty which prevent the establishment of a community.

You do not create a community by creating an organization and

59

saying there are community objectives. If the community does not exist, they will use the organization for selfish purposes in the name of principles stated in the Charter, and that I think is precisely what has happened....

What the United States Should Do

Obviously, this government faces hard problems. We romanticized the role of the United Nations and majority rule, especially when the Organization implemented American foreign policy. It will be extraordinarily difficult now to rationalize continued in-

"A HOUSE DIVIDED AGAINST ITSELF..."

Wood, courtesy of *Richmond New Leader*.

volvement in an Organization which sponsors wars, passes one-sided or unenforceable resolutions, provides forums for international insult instead of diplomacy, and is guilty of the most outrageous examples of selective justice. Perhaps it will be impossible for the American people to overcome disillusion and they will demand withdrawal from the world body. Because such action is inimical to our interests and those of world peace, I urge you,...to publicize honestly and soberly the reasons for our continued participation. By recognizing the United Nations as a dangerous weapon, you will be better able to discount its pernicious effects.

UN Only a Dream

Thirty years ago the U.N. began as the result of a dying President's dream to create an organization that would maintain world peace and help to usher in a new era of enlightenment. That the concept could never be more than a dream has, of course, been proven by events.

De Witt S. Copp, *Human Events*, May 29, 1976.

You will be less discouraged in your support for quiet diplomacy, mediation, efforts to avert nuclear or environmental catastrophes, and contribute better to social and economic justice for the peoples of the world. Clearer perception of the World Organization will facilitate the search for appropriate means of accomplishing these ends, which reality and good sense demand, and which must be pursued in spite of the uses made of the United Nations.

"If its influence is of no consequence or, indeed, negative, then the world may be better off without the U.N."

The United Nations Is Not Needed

Burton Yale Pines

Burton Yale Pines is a former associate editor at *Time* magazine and a three-time winner of the New York Newspaper Guild's Page One Award for outstanding reporting on domestic and foreign affairs. The author of *Back to Basics*, a book analyzing the conservative resurgence in the United States, he is presently vice president of research with The Heritage Foundation, a Washington, DC based organization which researches and publishes an extensive assortment of materials dealing with foreign and domestic issues. In the following viewpoint, Mr. Pines asserts that the United Nations has "betrayed the spirit and substance of its own Charter." Given this fact, he questions the continued viability of the world organization.

As you read, consider the following questions:

1. According to the author, why have most Americans become disillusioned with the United Nations?
2. Why does the author believe that the United Nations is against the free enterprise system?
3. According to the author, in what ways has the United Nations changed since its inception nearly two decades ago?

Burton Yale Pines, *A World Without A U.N.* Washington, DC: The Heritage Foundation, 1984. Reprinted with permission.

In 1959...a Gallup Poll found 87 percent of Americans convinced that the U.N. was doing a good job. By 1971, tens of millions of Americans were having second thoughts and Gallup found that only 35 percent gave the U.N. passing grades. This dropped to 30 percent in 1980. And in March 1981, a Roper Poll discovered that only a slim 10 percent of Americans viewed the U.N. as "highly effective" in carrying out its functions....

What has been prompting America's disillusion with the U.N. has been the growing feeling, based on solid fact, that the United Nations is an organization out of control. For one thing, it has become exceedingly anti-U.S., anti-West and anti-free enterprise. Much worse, it has been betraying the spirit and substance of its own Charter. It has not been helping those poor, needy, and threatened communities of the world which it was created to serve. Even a cursory review of the U.N. record reads as an indictment of an organization in violation of its own Charter and promise. It has failed as a peacekeeper and as a protector of human rights. Its record of caring for refugees is suspiciously spotty, ignoring those legions attempting to flee communist-ruled Viet Nam while allowing the Palestine Liberation Organization to turn refugee camps into armed garrisons. Inefficiency, cronyism, high pay, lavish expense accounts and even corruption and illiteracy have become the all too common characteristics of the Secretariat and other U.N. bureaucracies. Meantime, U.N. agencies in New York, Paris, Geneva and Vienna serve as a valuable cover for Soviet, East European, Cuban and other espionage services hostile to the West.

"House of Mirrors"

What the United Nations has come to resemble most is a House of Mirrors at an amusement park. Like a House of Mirrors, the U.N. distorts reality—exaggerating some things, diminishing others and obscuring most. But unlike a House of Mirrors the U.N.'s distortions, particularly in the General Assembly and the Secretariat, form a predictable pattern. One characteristic of this pattern is the U.N.'s politicization of issues that merely are technical. Certainly the behavior of Israel, Chile and South Africa are not really the most urgent issues confronting the General Assembly, to say nothing of the World Health Organization, UNESCO, the International Atomic Energy Agency and a host of other agencies. Yet issues related to these countries dominate the U.N. agenda. As a result, ostensibly technical U.N. bodies squander an enormous amount of time, resources, and energy dealing with a handful of political items forced onto their agendas by a bloc of nations strongly influenced by the Palestine Liberation Organization and other radical leftist groups and states.

Another aspect of the U.N.'s pattern of distortion is the globalization of problems. Bringing a local or even regional squabble to the General Assembly compels every nation to take a stand. Issues which could remain local suddenly gain global importance and therefore almost always become more difficult to resolve. Observed U.S. Permanent Representative to the United Nations Jeane Jordan Kirkpatrick in a 1982 address to the Anti-Defamation League: "Instead of being an effective instrument for conflict resolution, [the U.N.] serves all too often as an arena in which conflict is polarized, extended and exacerbated, in which differences are made deeper and more difficult to resolve than they would otherwise be."

Illegitimate Legitimacy

Dangerous too is the legitimacy conferred by the U.N. on the illegitimate, while discrediting those entitled to respect as members of the world community. Within the U.N. system, for example, the PLO and South West African People's Organization (SWAPO) enjoy near official status and are treated not as the terrorists that they are but as members in good standing of the international community. Israel, South Africa, Chile, and the Shah's Iran, meanwhile, are or have been reviled as pariah states.

Most dangerous, perhaps, is the U.N.'s crusade against the free enterprise system. In many respects, the U.N. has become the headquarters and strategic planning center of an anti-free enterprise campaign. In almost every U.N. body and almost always in the General Assembly, seldom is an opportunity lost to attack the free enterprise system. These assaults come as direct attacks on the Western industrial democracies which are the main capitalist nations. They come too as attacks on individual industries through increasing attempts to impose international codes of regulation.

Attack the US

Among the non-Marxist countries in the U.N., there seems to be an understanding—implicit more than explicit, but an understanding nevertheless—that a human right is whatever the U.N. declares to be one. This is why they work so hard to have resolutions adopted, and why they so sharply criticize the United States for sometimes voting against them or, worse, for refusing to ratify one of the covenants.

Walter Berns, *Public Opinion,* April/May 1983.

They come as attacks on the most successful of the capitalistic enterprises, the firm which has grown beyond the boundaries of the country in which it was founded and in which it is headquartered—the multinational corporation. And the U.N. crusade attacks the very essence and philosophical base of the free enterprise system. It is an assault which condemns, almost always without supporting evidence, the notion that the dynamo of growth and economic expansion is individual initiative, creativity and the incentive provided by the opportunity of making a profit. This kind of attack even repudiates the notion of economic growth, substituting for it the naive and economically self-defeating concepts of wealth redistribution and central planning.

The Gospel of NIEO

In repudiating free enterprise, and by ignoring capitalism's record of success, the United Nations and its agencies have raised to the level of gospel the tenets of what is called the New International Economic Order or, as it is widely known, NIEO. The tenacity with which the United Nations fights for NIEO at every forum, from every rostrum and in every possible publication and statement is awesome. Example: The United Nations Educational, Scientific and Cultural Organization (UNESCO) now deals with educational and cultural matters mainly as a means of promoting the NIEO agenda. Example: A U.N. conference ostensibly called to combat discrimination against women was transformed into a NIEO pep rally. This obsession with NIEO has converted the United Nations from an organization that might merely have been costly and annoying for Americans into a body which threatens those nations committed to democracy, liberty and economic development.

This raises the question, understandably, of whether the United Nations serves any positive purpose. If its influence is of no consequence or, indeed, negative, then the world may be better off without the U.N. At one time, to pose the matter in such a manner would have meant triggering a debate between competing theories of world order. Those who had faith in a U.N. would have been countered by those who lacked such faith. Today, however, the debate is not between competing theories, but is based on fact and history. The United Nations...no longer is simply a well-intentioned glimmer in an idealist's eye or an embryonic body whose missteps and failures understandably should be overlooked. It is a full-grown organization with a real record and history. A discussion of the U.N. and of whether the world would be better without it, therefore, now moves beyond theories and good intentions to a record comprised of facts and data, successes and failures....

Shift in Power

For nearly its first two decades, the United Nations mainly reflected the concerns of the world's industrial democracies. As new nations were formed and admitted to the U.N., in the wake of the dissolution of the world's empires (except that of the Soviet Union), the balance of power within the U.N. inexorably shifted. From 51 members in 1945, the U.N. grew to 82 by 1958, to 115 in 1964 and now stands at 158 member nations. While there is some merit to the argument that a global organization ought to have a universal membership, this has been translated simplistically into a policy within the U.N. (except for the Security Council) of one nation, one vote. As a result, policymaking is divorced from policy responsibility. A majority of today's U.N. members are ill-prepared to address the issues that come before the U.N., for these nations stand only on the threshold of political and economic development. They have no experience in international matters and can boast little knowledge of any history but that of their own transition from colonialism to independence. In almost every case, moreover, the majority of U.N. members have no respect for or faith in democracy. Yet they determine the policies that the U.N. adopts and which the United States and other democracies are obliged to execute and underwrite.

"The world would be the worse for its disappearance."

The United Nations Is Needed

Kurt Waldheim

Austrian born Kurt Waldheim has had a long and varied career as an international diplomat. An advocate of world peace through international cooperation, he held the influential post of secretary-general of the United Nations from January 1972 until January 1982. His most recent endeavor has been to attempt to form a lobbying group, composed of former world leaders, aimed at dealing with the world's critical prolems. In the following viewpoint, Mr. Waldheim maintains that the UN, despite its seeming failures, is one of the few potential paths to peace available in today's bellicose world. He concludes that the enlightened self-interest of all nations will ultimately provide the matrix the UN needs to establish international harmony.

As you read, consider the following questions:

1. Does the author believe that there is a problem reconciling "international peace" and "sovereign equality"? Why?
2. What does the author mean when he writes: "For many Europeans, the projection of the American dream into the international arena was a dangerous doctrine"?
3. According to the author, what are some of the accomplishments of the UN?

Kurt Waldheim, "The United Nations: The Tarnished Image," *Foreign Affairs*, Fall 1984. Reprinted with the author's permission.

In my last annual report as Secretary-General, I tried to assess the United Nations' ability to measure up to the new challenges of our times. "I have to say," I concluded, "that for all our efforts and our undoubted sincerity, the Organization has not yet managed to cut through the political habits and attitudes of earlier and less hurried centuries and to come to grips decisively with [the] new factors of our existence."

Indeed it has not. As a human political organization, the United Nations is certainly flawed. Its defects limit its capacity for effective action. In a mood of widespread disenchantment, it is attacked on the grounds that it produces more rhetoric than action, that it is ineffective and often ignored, and that the one-nation, one-vote system allows the Third World to dominate decision-making—divorcing voting power from the ability to act.

The system on paper is impressive. It has frequently helped to avoid or contain international violence. Yet in recent years it has seemed to cope less and less effectively with international conflicts of various kinds, and its capabilities in other areas of international cooperation have also seemed to dwindle.

But this is not to assert, as some do, that the United Nations is no longer a useful organization. Such critics use the wrong standard of comparison. The truly meaningful question regarding the United Nations is not whether it functions perfectly, or even rather poorly. It is whether humankind, taken as a whole, is better off with it or without it. As to that, it seems to me, there can be no doubt.

Founding of the UN

Depending on one's point of view, many explanations can be offered for the current state of affairs. To me, one factor is fundamental. The war syndrome is an inevitable outgrowth of the doctrine of state sovereignty. As long as states insist that they are the supreme arbiters of their destinies—that as sovereign entities their decisions are subject to no higher authority—international organizations will never be able to guarantee the maintenance of peace.

The statesmen who put together the United Nations at the end of World War II were quite aware of the need for some sort of supranational authority for an organization designed to prevent wars. But for understandable reasons they were unable, and indeed even unwilling, to make the radical changes needed to design a system that could be guaranteed to work. Accordingly, while the first *purpose* of the United Nations, as expressed in Article 1, paragraph 1 of its Charter, is "to maintain international peace and security...", the first *principle* of the Organization, as stated in Article 2, paragraph 1, is "...the sovereign equality of all its Members."

Limited by that constraint, the U.N. founding fathers went as far as they could to establish a system that would deter international conflict while it encouraged friendly relations among nations, and

68

economic growth and social progress through international cooperation. Essentially, the Organization they created operates through persuasion of sovereign states, not through compulsion. No substantive action of the U.N. General Assembly binds any member against its will, and the enforcement powers of the Security Council have remained almost unused. Thus, the United Nations enjoys strictly limited powers entirely disproportionate to the all-encompassing objectives it was created to seek. It is small wonder that many of these objectives remain beyond reach. It is because people do not know, or have forgotten, how little authority the United Nations actually has that they expect so much from it. In this sense it has been, as Americans are accustomed to say, "oversold."

America's Dream

Perhaps those who created the United Nations are open to the criticism that they led their peoples to expect too much from it, so that their disappointment is correspondingly greater. This point may be particularly applicable to Americans. In a sense, the United Nations is their own creation and the words of the Charter are in large part derived from the terminology of American political idealism.

Our Best Hope

The U.N. has its limitations, which were written into its charter from the beginning, with the right of the superpowers to veto its resolutions whenever they like. But even if Washington and Moscow could agree at Geneva on the control of nuclear weapons, each would still have enough of them to blow up the world, and all this world would be meaningless unless they finally accepted the first commitment of the U.N. Charter:

"All members shall refrain in their international relations from the threat or use of force against the territorial integrity or political independence of any state...."

No doubt it was a romantic ideal, but it's not quite fair for the nations that defied it to blame the United Nations, which still may be our best hope.

James Reston, *The New York Times*, November 12, 1983.

For many Europeans, the projection of the American dream into the international arena was a dangerous doctrine. They remembered Woodrow Wilson and the tide of emotional support for a new world order on which he arrived in Europe to make peace after the First World War. They recalled that in his noble naiveté he permitted himself to be used for the parochial interests so ably advanced by Lloyd George of Britain and Clemenceau of France. While assuring the birth of the League of Nations, he became a party to an inequitable peace treaty which helped to pave the way for the Germany of Adolf Hitler.

Europeans wonder whether, at the end of the Second World War, Franklin Roosevelt did not fall into the same trap, prepared for the practitioners of idealism by the practitioners of realism. For a Central European like myself, there is a parallel between the punitive settlement at Versailles in 1919 and the Yalta Conference in 1945. The division of the European continent at that time into two zones of influence, Eastern and Western, just as the ground rules for the U.N. Charter were being worked out, has had far-reaching, long-term effects, and many of our problems today grew out of this division....

Hard Days

No doubt this is a more direct, more simple, and more practical way for the Great Powers to do business. But these powers, under the U.N. Charter, have the principal responsibility for maintaining international peace and security, and the privileged voting position that goes with such a responsibility—the authority to block enforcement by veto. When they set such an example, who can blame other countries for pursuing the same course?...

The fact is plain. The United Nations has fallen upon hard days. It goes through its paces in a workaday routine that is increasingly ignored or condemned and that threatens to become increasingly irrelevant in the real world. Its vitality is being sapped. To some, its future is at best obscure. It is moving into fields of operation in which clashing interests threaten to tear it apart.

Let us try for perspective, for there are brighter elements in the picture. Forty years after its founding, the United Nations is more than ever a unique and universal organization. Unlike the League of Nations, it has not lost membership through withdrawals. It has not ceased to exist. Membership remains the badge of legitimacy for every newly independent country. The Organization can fairly take credit for having contributed in some crisis situations to the prevention of general war. When countries wish to use it, it can still serve as an instrument of peace—either as a safety valve for the venting of dangerous emotions or as a peacemaking/peacekeeping instrument for the containment of national rivalries. It is a meeting place for leaders and a crucible in which opposing conceptions of world order can be reconciled. The world would be the worse for its disappearance. And as a practical matter, it is just not possible realistically to expect its replacement by a better alternative.

To be sure, the habit of international cooperation is waning. In matters involving international security the trend is perfectly clear, but it is less evident in other fields. In large part this is because so much activity in the economic, social, human rights, and techno-

Peace is hell

logical fields continues without attracting much notice, in spite of its utility. But in these areas, too, the United Nations is now approaching zones of sensitivity that sharply pit members of different backgrounds against one another.

The new agenda, atop the ongoing debate over the New International Economic Order, raises complex problems of equity, ideology and conflicting interests. States enjoying a technological or an economic lead tend to view U.N. intervention with suspicion. The United States, for example, has rejected the Law of the Sea Treaty, laboriously crafted over a period of many years with the concurrence of U.S. delegations representing earlier American administrations. And the U.S. perception of the threat posed by the proposed New International Information Order was, in large part, responsible for the American announcement of its intention to withdraw from the United Nations Educational, Scientific and Cultural Organization. On its side, the Soviet Union continues to abstain from multilateral cooperation in the field of economic development.

A Recognizable Need

Nonetheless, I believe the enlightened self-interest of the nations should impel them to move in the right direction. I believe that sooner or later they will recognize the need for the single great world community—the interdependent world order—that is embodied in the Charter. They will learn to live together in a single global village, adjusting their differences and settling their common problems in a spirit of mutual accommodation.

For the superpowers this means following policies of détente and peaceful coexistence. For the North and the South, it means reaching across the chasm that separates the industrial and developing worlds for arrangements that will benefit them both. For states quarreling over territorial boundaries, it means a willingness to work for and accept compromise settlements, with the assistance, where needed, of disinterested third parties. In short, nations will have to learn to live within a pluralistic world system, integrated by an overriding interest in global peace and welfare. Because of these imperatives, I have an abiding faith in the survival of the United Nations.

"The end of the UN would in all likelihood lead to World War III."

The United Nations Is a Success

Douglas Mattern

Douglas Mattern is a writer and lecturer on world peace issues. A senior electronics engineer, he is currently codirector of the World Citizens Political Project, and secretary general of the World Citizens Assembly, both international peace organizations. In the following viewpoint, the author offers what he believes are some of the United Nations' positive accomplishments and outlines steps which he feels would increase its effectiveness.

As you read, consider the following questions:

1. According to the author, what was the most important problem which the creators of the UN failed to foresee?
2. What are some of the service agencies of the UN?
3. Does the author believe the United States has played a positive or negative role in the UN? Explain your answer.

Douglas Mattern, "The United Nations," *New Realities*, August 1983. Excerpted & condensed from *New Realities* magazine with permission. © NEW REALITIES MAGAZINE, 680 Beach Street, San Francisco, 94109.

Although often maligned, misunderstood, and even maliciously used as a scapegoat by governments and uninformed individuals, the United Nations remains the only pivotal global force to move toward the world community that is imperative for our civilization to survive and move forward to the 21st century....

The great theme of the Charter remains: "to save future generations from the scourge of war." However, regardless of the good will and the honest commitment during the creation of the UN Charter, no one could foresee the tremendous problems that would overtake the world and its new organization.

Most important was the "bomb" and subsequent dawning of the nuclear age, coming only two months after the Charter was signed. This was followed by another dramatic transition of modern history: the end of colonialism. Over the next decades the world would grow from some 60 nations to more than 160. It was an era that future historians will look back on as a time when hundreds of millions of people gained their freedom and independence after centuries of oppression and humility. It was an epic era, and the UN played a vital role, providing a world forum for new national leaders, a much needed training ground for new diplomats, and providing a focus for fast changing world events. Throughout this period, the UN accomplished the enormous feat of gaining universal membership: a true world organization in which—to some extent at least—all the peoples of the world are represented.

UN Agencies

From the beginning, a major role of the UN has been expressed through its specialized agencies, the largest section of the UN system which most Americans remain unaware of to this day, and yet which have served the interests of hundreds of millions of people throughout the globe. These agencies are:

- Food and Agriculture Organization (FAO)
- Inter-Government Maritime Consultative Organization (IMCO)
- International Bank for Reconstruction and Development (WORLD BANK)
- International Civil Aviation Organization (ICAO)
- International Development Association (IDA)
- International Finance Corporation (IFC)
- International Fund for Agricultural Development (IFAD)
- International Labor Organization (ILO)
- International Monetary Fund (IMF)
- International Telecommunications Union (ITU)
- UN Education Scientific and Cultural Organization (UNESCO)
- Universal Postal Union (UPU)
- World Health Organization (WHO)
- World Intellectual Property Organization (WIPO)
- World Meteorological Organization (WMO)
- UN Industrial Development Organization (UNIDO)

- International Atomic Energy Agency (IAEA)....

Some of the major world conferences initiated and sponsored by the UN include:

- 1968 UNESCO World Conference on the Biosphere (before ecology was a popular issue)
- 1972 UN World Conference on the Environment
- 1974 First World Conference on Population
- 1976 World Conference on Human Settlements
- 1977 First World Conference on Water (90% of the people in the developing countries [the majority of humankind] do not have safe drinking water)
- 1977 UN Conference on Agrarian Reform and Rural Development
- 1978 UN Special Session on Disarmament
- 1981 UN Conference on New and Renewable Resources of Energy
- 1982 World Conference on the Elderly
- 1982 Second UN Special Session on Disarmament (largest disarmament conference in history).

In 1982, the UN also completed the Law of the Sea Treaty after many long years of negotiation. Approved by 117 nations, this treaty attempts to ensure that all humanity will share in the future mining wealth of the oceans, and not simply the rich few. This treaty is a major step for the UN toward the transition to a global organization that can fulfill the best interests of all people....

UN Peacekeeping

The United Nations has played a major role in settling over 70 important peace-threatening disputes in the last 40 years. Today, peacekeeping forces help maintain stability in places like the Mid-East and Cyprus where, otherwise, violence would be likely. There have, of course, been wars. If two or more nations want to fight, the U.N. has no power to stop them. The U.N.'s principal function is to provide a forum for peaceful settlements of disputes.

Global Education Center, University of Minnesota, *Newsletter*, April 1985.

This is not to say, however, that everything the UN has attempted has been successful, or that all is good with the world organization. We must recognize that the UN reflects the real world as no other institution. And the real world is still burdened with prejudice, fear, greed, and other of the darker attributes of humanity. One of the great problems is that since the inception of the UN it has received competition from an even stronger force. This is the exaggerated nationalism that dominates global politics, and specifically, the cold war that has poisoned national policies for decades, and continues to do so today. These two related forces have spawned a militarism attitude that permeates our societies from economics to foreign policy.

It has led us to the present state of the world in which more than 50,000 nuclear weapons are stockpiled; estimated to equal 1.5 million Hiroshima bombs. But even with this incomprehensible overkill capability which has turned our planet into a ticking timebomb, we are being thrust into a new spiral of the nuclear arms race with weapons that are far more dangerous and destructive than existing ones. This danger centers on potential first-strike weapons, first-strike because they are being designed with extreme accuracy. This is not needed for any retaliation policy, but designed to destroy the other side's missiles in their silos—something possible only by attacking first (otherwise the silos would be empty). The bottom line is that the odds on a nuclear war starting by accident or miscalculation would increase dramatically.

Another tragic and unstable condition in our world is the overwhelming poverty which afflicts about 60 percent of humanity. This dire condition is partly the result of a huge population increase in the developing countries; partly the result of the ravages of colonialism which left most territories in shambles (which the Western world has yet to acknowledge); and partly due to the astronomical exhaustion of the world's wealth and resources on military programs. Today the nations collectively spend more than $1 million per minute on the military. Our own country now spends over $400,000 per minute, or $576 million a day, and if the current trend continues, we soon will be spending $1 *billion* per day on military programs.

One Problem

In 1982, the UN issued a comprehensive study on the relationship of disarmament to development and concluded that "The arms race and underdevelopment are not two problems: they are one. They must be solved together, or neither will ever be solved. The world can either continue to indulge in an arms race with characteristic vigour, or make deliberate attempts to establish a more sustainable international economic and political order. It cannot do both."

To understand this analysis we need only review global grim statistics: 700 million people suffer from severe malnutrition... 800 million people are illiterate...30 percent of the children in the developing countries die before the age of five due to malnutrition and disease...250 million children do not go to school...1.5 billion people have little or no medical care...40 countries are so poor they have to beg for food...the World Bank reports that the condition of the majority of children in the world is "depressing."

Another statistic that underlies what is wrong with the priorities of our civilization is that the world spends an average of $16,000 each year per soldier and $260 for education per child. Perhaps more dramatic is that each year military programs cost every man, woman and child an average of about $100, while the average for all UN programs is 57¢ and for international peacekeeping the total is 5¢. In summary, the world spends about 2000 times more for military purposes than for attempts at peacekeeping, and we now have more pounds of explosives per person than food.

A wise man once said the opposite of love is not hate, but apathy. And it has been apathy that allowed us to reach the current state of danger and confused priorities. For example, Americans know hardly anything about the daily constructive work of the UN because the U.S. media ignores it, preferring to concentrate mainly on the negative aspects.

UN Accomplishments

In human rights, the law of the sea, womens' issues, and the problem of racial discrimination, the U.N. has been helpful in establishing new norms of international law. There may be some sensationalism in the press in playing up the failures of the United Nations and instances of defeat by the United States. The press loves to report the extraordinary and the unusual rather than what is routine and customary.

Yasushi Akashi, *The Churchman*, October 1984.

There has also been a deteriorating vision: a narrowing of a global perspective that has reached a new low through the attitude and policies of our government. In mid-December the UN General Assembly presented 25 major resolutions designed to curb the nuclear arms race. Our government rejected 21 of them. This included a proposal for an immediate nuclear freeze and a resolution to ban further testing of nuclear warheads. Both were passed by overwhelming margins with the U.S. in a small minority. In fact the resolution on banning nuclear tests passed by a 111-1 margin, with the U.S. casting the lone negative vote. The Law of the Sea Treaty, mentioned earlier, was adopted by a 117-4 vote, with the U.S. in the tiny minority. These figures alone reveal the task to achieve a major change in world events begins right here at home.

Remember the League

There are individuals and organizations who claim we need to ignore the UN, even do away with it. History reminds that this would be both foolish and disastrous. The demise of the League of Nations soon led to World War II: the end of the UN would in all likelihood lead to World War III.

The reality is that *no* real progress can occur without a major shift in attitudes, priorities, and a more comprehensive global perspective among active people and their governments. As Albert Einstein stated: "The unleashed power of the atom has changed everything save our modes of thinking, and thus we drift toward unparalleled catastrophe...a new type of thinking is essential if mankind is to survive and move toward higher levels."

It is true that the UN needs some changes, both in structure, charter, and in a renewed sense of idealism and hope. But we should remember that the UN Charter was not etched in stone, never meant not to be amended. We need only review the views of the primary architect, Franklin D. Roosevelt. When commenting on the San Francisco Conference to draft the charter, Roosevelt said: "No plan is perfect. Whatever is adopted at San Francisco will doubtless have to be amended time and again over the years, just as our own constitution has been. No one can say exactly how long any plan will last. Peace can endure only so long as humanity really insists upon it, and is willing to work for it, and to sacrifice for it."...

Steps to Be Taken

Some practical steps to improve the effectiveness of the UN within the political arena have been set by the U.S. based Campaign for UN Reform:

1. Creation of an International Disarmament Organization under the UN system to initiate and monitor a nuclear freeze, arms limitation and step-by-step phased reduction disarmament agreements and, most importantly, to verify each nation's compliance.

2. Creation of a highly trained UN Conciliation and Mediation Service to enhance the dispute settlement process. This service would mediate international disputes by making available panels of arbitrators to render non-binding or binding decisions on disputes and enable the Security Council to request binding arbitration when international peace and security are threatened.

3. Establishment of a Permanent UN Peacekeeping Force as provided for in the Charter. This must be of sufficient size and mobility to maintain the status quo while UN dispute settlement procedures are taking place.

It would be useful for a code of principles to be established at the UN for those privileged to serve, whether as permanent members of the Secretariat and UN agencies, or as national representatives. Let us never forget that the opening words to the preamble of the Charter states "We the people...." The representatives thereby serve more than their specific jobs or national governments, but humanity as a whole.

===

"Even an imbecile can see the [UN] isn't working."

===

The United Nations Is a Failure

Richard Grenier

Richard Grenier is a professional writer whose works include both fiction and nonfiction. One of his novels, *The Marrakesh One-Two,* was nominated for the National Book Critics Circle Award. In the following viewpoint, Mr. Grenier delivers a bitter indictment of the UN, categorizing it as hypocritical and menacing in its actions.

As you read, consider the following questions:

1. What did Sir Harold Nicolson write about the United Nations?
2. What does the author mean when he writes that the United Nations has become a "third-world club"?
3. According to the author, in what ways is the United Nations highly selective in its support of violence?
4. What does the author believe would happen if the United States withdrew from the United Nations?

When the United Nations was founded in San Francisco in June 1945, its principal purpose, recorded in the opening line of the preamble to the organization's charter, was "to save succeeding generations from the scourge of war." Since that time the world has seen more than one hundred armed conflicts, including some forty major wars, which have killed over ten million people. Even an imbecile can see the place isn't working....

Origins of the UN

We owe the most lucid and simple analysis of the "grand fallacy" of the United Nations to Sir Harold Nicolson of Britain. Nicolson, whose experience of world affairs was probably greater than that of the whole U.S. delegation put together, explained that the U.N. "began with the idea that one could and should apply to external affairs the institutions and practices of legislative procedure in a liberal democracy." What was expected in San Francisco, he noted with some incredulity, was that all these peace-loving peoples (the war-loving peoples having been suppressed forever) would meet and by debate and majority vote decide what was reasonable and right. Violence would be superseded by reason. People would no longer make war on or bully a neighboring people, it seemed, because it was so unreasonable and their mutual love of peace so great. (Would the people of Massachusetts make war on the people of Connecticut?) And thus war—unreasonable and brutish by its very nature—would disappear from the face of the earth.

But it somehow escaped the attention of most of the 282 delegates, 1,444 assistants, 1,589 members of the new Secretariat, 2,636 journalists, 800 Boy Scouts, and 400 Red Cross workers who toiled so mightily in San Francisco to save succeeding generations from the scourge of war that what applied to Massachusetts and Connecticut might not apply, for example, to Libya and Chad. When...Libyan troops invaded Chad in a classic act of international aggression without a shred of propaganda rationalization, the matter didn't even generate enough interest to cause a resolution to be drafted (let alone approved) by that holy of holies, the U.N. Security Council.

Mind you, the otherworldly fog that enveloped San Francisco in those first days began to dissipate rather rapidly—within months— when it became clear that the lands occupied by the Red Army during World War II, from Petsamo to the Kuriles, would never get a chance to be Connecticut, or, for that matter, even Chad. But this, to be frank, did not disturb Washington overmuch. Even if the U.N. was not going to be the Kingdom of God envisioned in its charter, America was going to run it; which it proceeded to do. To support the U.N. in those days—and I would say this lasted for some twenty years—was to support the United States as an internationalist world power, to support the containment of communism and, indeed, to support American policy everywhere. Hard-nosed pragmatism supplanted starry-eyed idealism, though no one explained to the American people that the United Nations itself was based on preposterous assumptions about the world, even about the nature of man, and that it might someday fall into the hands of bad-type people, who might not only reduce it to impotence but use it to do a lot of mischief. For the time being we ran it, and that was enough.

Declining American Influence

We don't run it any longer. Some analysts feel that the watershed year was 1960, when a bumper crop of seventeen new members was admitted, raising the membership from eighty-three to one hundred. All of them were former colonies of once great European empires; none of them was a democracy. But if the position of America and the West deteriorated steadily during the '60s, it became a rout in the '70s. Rightly or wrongly (I would guess wrongly), the U.S. had fought to the end to keep communist China out of the United Nations, preserving the "Chinese" seat—and above all the permanent Chinese membership (and veto power) in the Security Council—for Taiwan. In 1971 there was a battle royal. Washington lost. The People's Republic of China (with which, curiously enough, we were soon to have excellent relations) took over the Chinese seat. But American power in the U.N. was broken, probably forever.

UN May Diminish Peace

The U.N. has enjoyed some success in peace-maintenance, particularly in the prevention of escalation and in helping parties to a dispute to disengage. Although nuclear war has been avoided, this is due more to NATO's deterrence policy than efforts in the U.N. Moreover, a reluctance on the U.N.'s part to recognize or address the reality of Soviet expansionist policy, coupled with disarmament proposals that may undermine deterrence, could diminish rather than strengthen the preservation of peace in the future.

Maurice Tugwell, *A World Without a U.N.*, 1984.

The United Nations now has 158 members, more than triple its original membership. Its latest admission is St. Kitts-Nevis, two islands in the Caribbean with a total population of 65,000—two thirds that of Sioux City, Iowa. I will spare you Vanuatu, Fiji, and the Seychelles. Washington now pays, by assessment, 25 percent of the official budget of the United Nations, and perhaps one third of all real U.N. expenditures (the U.N. Secretariat has never been able to determine the exact figure), whereas the seventy-two nations who voted for the "Zionism is racism" resolution in the General Assembly pay an average of about one third of one percent apiece. In the United Nations, it is obviously not one dollar, one vote. More interestingly, it is not one man, one vote either. Africa, for example, has only 10 percent of the world's population. But the African bloc at the U.N., because of the continent's political fragmentation, accounts for a full third of the U.N. membership. China (one vote) has more than twice the population of all of Africa.

A Third-World Club

The United Nations has become, in short, a third-world club. It is a glass house filled with elegantly turned-out and inordinately highly paid delegates from impoverished, nondemocratic countries who on every public occasion pour the most vitriolic abuse on the Western democratic nations that gave the organization birth, and under whose lofty principles it supposedly still meets. The U.N. is often called a mere debating society, a "bag of wind." I think this is flattery. What emerges from that immense tower on the shore of the East River is not just a harmless, if noisy, passing wind. By setting the agenda for world debate, and hammering away at many demagogical idées fixes, this organization is responsible for a lot of mischief at loose in the world today.

Perhaps thirty members of the United Nations represent democratic societies of proven stability. Applying the criteria of Freedom House to determine what is a democracy and what is not, another twenty-five members make the grade today, though who knows in what column they will be tomorrow. (Nigeria is just taking its first baby steps as a democracy, and Lord knows I wish it well.) Most of the 100-odd members of this "parliament of man" represent countries that, back home, are naked autocracies. In other words, we have here an organization devoted to peace between neighbors whose members routinely practice war on their citizens. What kind of peace-loving governments are these? When their delegates meet in Manhattan it is rather like a group of Mafia family chieftains gathered for a "peace conference" in upstate New York. Actually, this metaphor might be unfair—to the Mafia. Mafiosi, at least, do not make endless high-sounding speeches about global peace and justice.

Since the evaporation of American primacy, the United Nations—and I mean the Security Council almost as much as the zoo-like General Assembly—has been controlled by a system of blocs. We have the Soviet bloc, of course, which now includes South Yemen, Ethiopia, Angola, Mozambique, and quite a few others. But more important, we have the African bloc, the Arab bloc, the Latin American bloc, the Islamic Conference (some overlapping), and a really dynamite bloc you have probably never heard of (because it amounts to so little) called WEOG. Now on the face of it, it is somewhat odd that WEOG is such a contemptible bloc at Turtle Bay, because WEOG stands for "Western European and Other States Group" and its members include many of the world's richest and most powerful nations, even Japan.

© 1986 McNaught Syndicate. Reprinted with permission.

The two greatest blocs at the United Nations, however, are the "Group of 77," so called because it has 126 members, and the "Non-Aligned Movement," so called because of its systematic hostility to the West. These two groups do more than overlap; they are essentially the same group wearing two hats. When the Third World wants to powwow for economic purposes it calls itself the Group of 77 (in U.N.-ese, "G-77"). When it wants to powwow for political purposes it calls itself the Non-Aligned Movement (in U.N.-ese, "NAM"). Last year's president of the Non-Aligned Movement was Cuba, which was accorded the customary courtesy of drawing up the agenda and drafting the original version of all the Movement's proposals, initiatives, and resolutions. This must have been great fun for such a nonaligned person as Fidel Castro, whose nonaligned island is the base for a Soviet combat brigade. But once the sanctified U.N. nomenclature is breached, who knows what might happen next? The whole glass house might come tumbling down. Cuba was succeeded this year by India, which was the first country outside the Warsaw Pact to recognize the Vietnamese puppet regime in Cambodia, has refused to condemn the Soviet Union for invading Afghanistan, and, most recently, refused to condemn the Soviet Union for shooting down the South Korean airliner.

Now these third-world "blocs" that run the United Nations are highly fissiparous, or, put otherwise, have hardly any real existence in the outside world. Witness the murderous relationships between Syria and Iraq, Libya and Egypt, Morocco and Algeria (Polisario), not to mention the—yes—ninety-six contending *domestic* militias in Lebanon. As for the Islamic Conference, witness the three-year war still going on between Iraq and Iran, in which the toll of dead has reached an estimated 200,000. The "African bloc" is probably the most disciplined by the time it gets to Manhattan, but Ethiopia and Somalia are still fighting over the Ogaden. Five years ago an army from Tanzania invaded Uganda with the worthy purpose of overthrowing the notorious Idi Amin and incidentally setting up a new government sympathetic to Tanzania, but word of the invasion never seemed to reach Manhattan. Idi Amin, now living comfortably in Saudi Arabia, is not one of nature's nobleman, but the function of the United Nations is to prevent wars and invasions among sovereign, national states. It was never intended to issue free hunting licenses to countries wanting to make war for laudable purposes, even overthrowing Idi Amin or Pol Pot.

The Israeli Factor

The African bloc, so solid at Turtle Bay, is actually a highly variegated group, and when governments deal with these countries individually they often get surprisingly good results. But when the bloc caucuses it reaches for some kind of lowest common denominator, which is, of course, hostility to racist South Africa. Now, every state in black Africa is filled with tribal animosities, and often with racial discrimination. A few years back the Tutsi of Burundi, a Nilotic people and a "master race" physically very distinct from their Hutu serfs, found the Hutu were getting a little uppity and exterminated some 200,000 of them *pour encourager les autres.* It was all a domestic affair, just a little intramural squabble that did not disturb the international order. Few people have even heard of it, although it is in the standard reference books. But I ask the reader to imagine the world reaction if white South Africa had tried any such trick against its black population.

The Arab bloc's lowest common denominator is Israel. The two groups caucus and meet annually in the Conference of Non-Aligned Nations. By the time these "non-aligned" nations arrive at Turtle Bay, they are ready to steamroller all opposition in the General Assembly. That, incidentally, is the true meaning of the "Zionism [Israel] is racism [South Africa]" resolution—the United Nations is now controlled by an Arab-African coalition, with the blessing of the Soviet Union....

The United Nations is an organization that actively supports the violent overthrow of sovereign states by revolutionary movements. But not all states and not all movements. It is highly selective. To qualify, a movement must be radical and Marxist, and, of course, terrorists are welcome. In 1970 the U.N. General Assembly approved a resolution encouraging "colonial peoples" and national liberation movements to use "all necessary means at their disposal" to overthrow sovereign governments. In 1974 Yasir Arafat of the PLO, pistol on his hip, received a standing ovation when he addressed the General Assembly. The PLO and SWAPO (the Marxist-terrorist "South West Africa People's Organization") are now not only official "permanent observers" at the United Nations, they are partly funded by it. Since 1977 SWAPO has been granted an estimated $40 million of U.N. money, and a pro-PLO "Division for Palestinian Rights" has spent more than $6 million. The PLO—get this—took part in a U.N. conference on civil aviation and airplane hijacking. The ANC and PAC, communist-dominated guerrilla and terrorist groups operating across the South African border, receive a biannual U.N. subsidy of at least $9 million. The major nonviolent black opposition to the South African government, however, is the Inkatha, led by the head of the Zulu Nation. It receives no U.N. support.

Soviet Arrogance

Soviet arrogance was most eloquently illustrated in the fall of 1979. Even as they were finalizing plans for the brutal invasion of Afghanistan, the Russians engineered a resolution, pushed through the General Assembly by Third World delegates, which in its final form "resolutely condemns policies of pressure and use, or threat of use, of force, direct or indirect aggression, occupation and the growing practice of interference, overt or covert, in the internal affairs of states." Exactly one month later, the Russians were firmly in Afghanistan.

Ralph Kinney Bennett, *Reader's Digest*, October 1983.

Notice the odd concentration of U.N. activity around the organization's two pariah states, South Africa and Israel, as if they were the only trouble spots on the globe. In the *Through the Looking Glass* world of the U.N., words mean only what the U.N. says they mean. I have no idea why the Afghans struggling desperately to free their country from Soviet occupation do not qualify as a national liberation movement, but I have never heard them mentioned once in the corridors of the U.N., except by the United States. Nor have I ever heard talk of the Kurds, who have been fighting everyone around them for generations. And again, except from the U.S., I have never heard a whisper about such obvious non-nations as Poland, Czechoslovakia, Hungary, Estonia, Latvia, Lithuania, Moldavia, Uzbekistan, Kirghizia...but you know the list. Or do you?...

Other functions of the United Nations are menacing, if not openly bellicose. With the 260 members of the Soviet U.N. delegation and the 250 Soviet citizens employed by the U.N. Secretariat, New York is the key center for Soviet espionage in the United States, a simple proof of which is that Vladimir Kazakov, KGB station chief at the Soviet mission, is the former head of the American Department of the KGB in Moscow. Gennadi Yevstavyev, special assistant to U.N. Secretary General Pérez de Cuéllar, is also an officer of the KGB. The "New World economic order," now totally espoused by the United Nations, is systematically and relentlessly anti-Western and "redistributionist."

During the...flap over the Korean airline massacre, many Americans asked if the U.N. should get out of New York. The more profound question is whether or not the U.S. should get out of the United Nations....

The Primary Issue

As one very high official in the administration remarked to me, the primary issue is whether with us out, the U.N. could become even more dangerous for us than it already is. Do we serve to brake its anti-Western extremism? Without us, would it become an even more effective tool of our adversaries? But another very high official in the administration feels that the presence of America in the United Nations gives the organization one of the principal claims to legitimacy it now possesses, and that without us it would stand revealed as the third-world Soviet lynch mob it has become, diplomatically useless, in consequence, to these very parties. With us out, our Western allies would soon follow, he feels, along with many pro-Western countries in the Third World (some of which have already defected from the "Non-Aligned Movement"), and the United Nations would soon collapse.

Would such a radical course lead to a breakdown in international affairs and threaten world peace? Well, as George Kennan once wrote, the difficulty of a negotiation varies directly with the square of the number of parties participating. Since the square of 158 is 24,964, this would suggest that the U.N.'s value as a forum for negotiations is vastly overrated.

a critical thinking skill

Evaluating Sources of Information

A critical thinker must always question sources of information. Historians, for example, usually distinguish between *primary sources (eyewitness accounts)* and *secondary sources (writings or statements based on primary or eyewitness accounts or on other secondary sources.)* A speech by the United Nations Secretary General is an example of a primary account. An article by a journalist describing that speech is a secondary source.

In order to read and think critically, one must be able to recognize primary sources. However, this is not enough. Eyewitness accounts do not always provide accurate descriptions. Historians may find ten different eyewitness accounts of an event and all the accounts might interpret the event differently. The historians must then decide which of these accounts provide the most objective and accurate interpretations.

Test your skill in evaluating sources of information by completing the following exercise. Pretend that your teacher tells you to write a research report about whether or not the United Nations is an effective world peace organization. You decide to include an equal number of primary and secondary sources. Listed below are a number of sources which may be useful in your research. Carefully evaluate each of them. *Then, place a P next to those descriptions you believe are primary sources. Second, rank the primary sources assigning the number (1) to what appears to be the most objective and accurate primary source, the number (2) to the next most objective, and so on until the ranking is finished. Repeat the entire procedure, this time placing an S next to those descriptions you feel would serve as secondary sources and then ranking them.*

If you are doing this activity as a member of a class or group, discuss and compare your evaluation with other members of the group. If you are reading this book alone, you may want to ask others if they agree with your evaluation. You will probably discover that others will come to different conclusions than you. Listening to their reasons may give you valuable insights in evaluating sources of information.

P = *primary*
S = *secondary*

1. a copy of the United Nations Charter

2. a book titled *The United Nations: 1945 to the Present*

3. a letter from President Roosevelt to Winston Churchill regarding the formation of a post-war organization to insure peace

4. an article about the effectiveness of the UN by a professor of political science at a well-known university

5. a biography of Dag Hammarskjöld, a prominent former secretary-general of the UN.

6. a television interview with the German delegate to the General Assembly

7. an autobiography of Kurt Waldheim, a prominent former UN secretary-general.

8. a college student's research paper on the UN's role in Korea

9. a map indicating areas where UN peacekeeping forces are or have been stationed

10. a pamphlet on UN achievements in supplying food to the hungry

11. a newspaper article reporting on a meeting of the Security Council in New York

12. a chapter about the UN in a book on Soviet-American relations

13. viewpoint two from this chapter

14. an interview with President Reagan in which he outlines his hopes for the future of the UN

15. minutes of a General Assembly meeting

16. an editorial about the UN's role in Syria by an accountant in Chicago

17. a transcript of an unofficial meeting between the delegates of the five permanent nations in the Security Council

18. a televised debate between two US senators in which they discuss the effect of the UN on American interests

Bibliography

The following list of books, periodicals, and pamphlets deals with the subject matter of this chapter.

Yasushi Akashi	"U.N. Resolve," *Harper's*, March 1984.
Ralph Kinney Bennett	"The Broken Promise of the United Nations," *Reader's Digest*, October 1983.
Walter Berns	"Taking the United Nations Seriously," *Public Opinion*, April/May 1983.
Kevin Bryant	"How to Bring Attention to the Non-political Aspects of the United Nations," *The Humanist*, April/May 1984.
Javier Perez de Cuellar	"The U.N. 'Simply Must Be Made to Succeed,'" *The New York Times*, October 20, 1985.
Thomas G. Gulick	"The U.N.'s War Against the West," *Human Events*, February 16, 1985.
Gene H. Hogberg	"The United Nations After 40 Years: The Original Signers Speak Out," *The Plain Truth*, October 1985.
Don Kirk	"UN's Critics in the US: It's Them Against Us," *USA Today*, September 25, 1985.
Jeane J. Kirkpatrick	"The United Nations as a Political System: A Practicing Political Scientist's Insights into U.N. Politics," *American Foreign Policy Newsletter*, October 1983.
Tommy T.B. Kon	"The United Nations: Is There Life After 40?" *USA Today*, September 1985.
Robert W. Lee	"The UN Reality Versus the Modern Cliches," *The New American*, October 28, 1985.
Charles William Maynes	"A Cause Worth Fighting For," *The Nation*, September 21, 1985.
The New York Times	"Three Yesses for the U.N.," October 24, 1985.
Burton Yale Pines	*A World Without a U.N.* Washington, DC: The Heritage Foundation, 1984.
Vernon A. Walters	"The United Nations a Force for Peace?" *American Legion Magazine*, December 1985.

International Monetary Organizations

Internationalism

Introduction

The United States emerged from World War II economically stronger than when it had entered the war. Its size and vast resources were partially responsible for this. But perhaps more important was the fact that its land was not directly touched by the destructive maelstrom of battle. Most of war-torn Europe and Asia, however, were not as fortunate. Drained by the costs of war, the world anticipated economic dislocation that would become pandemic. The world economic situation following World War I had been dire and catastrophic and offered a lesson not to be ignored. Thus, in 1944 representatives from forty-four nations conceived a partial solution. They created the World Bank and the International Monetary Fund.

The World Bank's official name (International Bank for Reconstruction and Development) explains its purpose well. Funded by the governments of developing countries and by private investors, it is an international organization through which countries needing aid for development can obtain loans. The International Monetary Fund (IMF), funded by contributions from member nations, was orginally established to maintain economic stability and balanced trade between nations. Although there are other international monetary organizations which also aid in development, these two are among the most influential and controversial.

Over time, the functions of the World Bank and the IMF have become more and more similar. Both organizations represent an attempt at international cooperation to solve world monetary problems. Both lend money to countries wanting aid for development. While the IMF traditionally has been a source of loans for extreme emergencies and has placed much more stringent requirements upon the recipients, many authorities today believe that the World Bank is also heading in this direction.

The authors of the viewpoints in this chapter debate the question of whether or not these international organizations actually work the way they are supposed to. That is, do they really aid poor or less developed nations, and, by so doing, help maintain world economic stability?

"The full range of Bank projects is intended to ease the painful existence of the poorest of the world's poor."

The World Bank Aids the Poor

Lewis M. Simons

In 1973, Robert McNamara assumed the presidency of the World Bank. Under his leadership, the primary goal of the bank became national development programs to assist the world's poor. The following viewpoint is taken from a report on the World Bank which was published in *Smithsonian* magazine. Lewis M. Simons, the author, is a *Washington Post* reporter who spent ten years as a correspondent in Asia. In the viewpoint, Mr. Simons points out some of the ways the World Bank has achieved its goal of benefiting the poor.

As you read, consider the following questions:

1. What are some examples the author cites showing that the World Bank has aided the poor?
2. According to the author, has eliminating poverty always been the primary goal of the bank?
3. How does the author demonstrate that, although the bank aims to help the poor, it is not a charity?

Lewis M. Simons, "From Quito to Delhi," *Smithsonian*, June 1981. Reprinted with the author's permission.

If you were an Indian farmer earning, say, $185 a year by growing wheat on a postage-stamp-size plot in the harsh, red earth of Rajasthan, what chance might you have of borrowing $1,200 from your local bank to put in a life-saving irrigation system?

The answer is no chance at all. If you could find a bank, it would hardly take your request seriously. Your farm, as it is, is virtually sterile. And, except for the land, you can offer the banker nothing as security.

But if your plight were shared by enough of your neighbors, and it caught the imagination of a local official, the government might eventually seek a multi-million-dollar loan from the World Bank, 10,000 miles away in Washington. A nod from this center of power would provide enough money to finance a major irrigation project, helping not just a single poor farmer, but thousands of his neighbors as well. Such a nod is given often enough. The World Bank is a busy place, the largest and most powerful government-to-government development institution in history....

Lending to Help Millions

Lending to help thousands or even millions is what the World Bank is all about; not savings or checking accounts, but money for world development. It is a system involving billions of dollars, more than a hundred countries and seemingly endless reports and statistics. But the bottom line is always people. In its 35 years of operation, the World Bank's $85 billion in loans for about 3,000 projects has enabled some of the world's poorest countries to help farmers like those in Rajasthan irrigate their crops, to build fertilizer plants and use new chemicals; to bring pure drinking water to peasants who had lived all their lives accepting intestinal diseases as a fact of life; to rehabilitate fetid city slums; to bring the blessings of electricity to darkened villages; to educate couples on why and how to limit the numbers of children they have; to build schools and help teachers to teach; to show mothers steeped in centuries of myth and ignorance how to care for their children better.

Although Bank lending accounts for only five to ten percent of the flow of long- and medium-term capital to developing countries, the prestige of the Bank is such that its thumbs-up or thumbs-down on a particular country or type of project has enormous influence on other prospective lenders or industrial firms. In a very real sense, the World Bank's decisions affect the economies of nations and the lives of millions.

A current example of huge scale is the Bank's entry into the field of oil and gas development and exploration. The decision to beef up its lending in these areas should ease the energy bite on many of the world's poorest nations, those whose economies have been damaged more by rocketing oil prices than by any other factor. As a start, the Bank plans loans of $1.2 billion a year by 1983 for 38 petroleum projects which, by maturity in 1990, are projected to produce 1.4 million barrels of oil a day. (For comparison, Saudi Arabia now produces 10.3 million barrels a day.)

Easing Painful Existence of the Poor

But oil exploration is only one of its development arms. Taken together, the full range of Bank projects is intended to ease the painful existence of the poorest of the world's poor, the more than 800 million people the Bank refers to as living in "absolute poverty."

To understand, you must see some of your fellow humans suffering daily on the streets of Calcutta, in the villages of Bangladesh or the parched settlements of sub-Saharan Africa. I remember the first time I saw entire families living in packing crates and storm pipes along stinking sewer canals in Djakarta. That was 1968. A decade later some still existed this way, but many had moved into little concrete-block houses built with assistance from the World Bank. A resident named Abu Jashid told me that the greatest boon was the simple cement drains that assured that human waste no longer mixed with drinking water.

Alleviation of Poverty

A key and central aim of The World Bank is the alleviation of poverty. Our objective in any developing country—anywhere in the world—is precisely the same: to assist the country both to accelerate its economic growth, and to reduce its level of domestic poverty by enhancing the productivity of its poor, and thus making possible a better standard of living for all its people.

A.W. Clausen, in a speech, September 6, 1982.

It is on people like Jashid that the World Bank has turned its beacon in the last decade. [Former] Bank president Robert S. McNamara signaled the new direction in lending in a speech before the Bank's board of governors in Nairobi on September 24, 1973.

"We plan to place far greater emphasis on policies and projects which will begin to attack the problems of absolute poverty," McNamara told the board. He explained that the bulk of the 800 million poorest, those surviving on 30 cents a day, lived in the rural sections of their countries.

No Trickle-Down

Until that rather dramatic moment in Nairobi, the World Bank, like most aid-giving institutions and governments, had concentrated on large-scale infrastructural projects: building hydroelectric plants, roads and railways, modernizing industry, boosting production for export. The theory most commonly held through the mid-1970s was that development of the modern sector would produce a "percolator" effect, eventually reaching the poorest.

But the economic theorists found that their plans didn't work like a coffeepot. Even though, in some cases, gross national product (GNP) rose as the rate of industrialization picked up, the plight of the subsistence farmers didn't improve. In fact, the net effect was to better the lives of relatively small numbers of city dwellers and industrial workers, as well as the wealthier landowners and big farmers....

It wasn't by accident (although hindsight reveals grave misjudgments) that the World Bank spent the first quarter-century of its existence concentrating on large-scale infrastructural projects. The founding fathers of the Bank, when they met at Bretton Woods, New Hampshire, in July 1944, while World War II was still raging, intended that the Bank would first turn to repairing war damage and then to making development loans based on sound economic policies.

Thus, the representatives of 44 nations at Bretton Woods named the new institution the International Bank for Reconstruction and Development (IBRD). Founded at the same time was the International Monetary Fund (IMF), to facilitate the freeing of international payments and international trade from restrictions. John Maynard Keynes, the acclaimed British economist, told the delegates: "It is likely, in my judgment, that the field of reconstruction from the consequences of war will mainly occupy the proposed Bank in its early days. But as soon as possible, and with increasing emphasis as time goes on, there is a second primary duty laid upon it, namely to develop the resources and productive capacity of the world, with special reference to the less developed countries."...

Not Charity

Despite the World Bank's aim to help the poor, it is not an institution based on charity, as many think, but a highly successful, conservatively managed, capitalistic institution....

Although it lends for many social projects that commercial lending institutions wouldn't touch, the World Bank has a record of repayment unparalleled in the banking community: not a single loan has ever been defaulted on. Why? We're a tougher, better and more effective lender than commercial banks," says [bank officer Eugene] Rotberg. "We don't reschedule loans. If a borrower is 30 days late, every country in the world is notified. If they're 60 days late, we put it in our prospectus. That places a certain subtle pressure on them." But, for obvious reasons, most borrowers maintain impeccable relations with the Bank.

Under this tough financial stewardship the Bank turns a handsome profit each year, and it's rising impressively: $238 million in 1978, $407 million in 1979 and $588 million in 1980. All profits are plowed back for use as loans or IDA credits.

95

"Studies of the impact of...aid programs on the rural poor majority in the Third World show that rather than 'helping the small farmer,'...aid programs support regimes that repress the poor and neglect their needs."

The World Bank Does Not Aid the Poor

David Kinley, Arnold Levinson, and Frances Moore Lappe

Critics of the World Bank argue that the billions of dollars it loans to developing countries do little to help the lives of the poor. Instead, these monies aid corrupt, often repressive governments of the developing countries and line the pockets of the capitalist countries which are the largest supporters of the bank. The authors of the following viewpoint concur with this negative opinion of the bank. David Kinley coordinates the aid education project of the Institute for Food and Development Policy in San Francisco. With Frances Moore Lappe and a third writer, he coauthored the book *Aid as Obstacle: Twenty Questions About Our Foreign Aid and the Hungry*. Arnold Levinson is a freelance writer/journalist based in Oakland, California.

As you read, consider the following qustions:

1. What are some examples cited by the authors to show that development money aids the rich and not the poor?
2. In the authors' opinion, what is the bank's primary concern?

David Kinley, Arnold Levinson, and Frances Moore Lappe, "The Myth of 'Humanitarian' Foreign Aid," *The Nation*, July 11, 1981. Reprinted with permission, *The Nation* magazine, National Associates, Inc. © 1981.

Studies of the impact of...aid programs on the rural poor majority in the Third World show that rather than "helping the small farmer," as claimed, bilateral and multilateral aid programs support regimes that repress the poor and neglect their needs, and mainly assist urban-oriented industrial and commercial development along with the rural "infrastructures" that serve it. Agricultural development programs are confined to the already better-off farmers, while neglecting the genuinely needy smallholders and landless, who compose the bulk of the rural poor. The World Bank's aid...goes to governments, not people, let alone the poor. And its lending is so concentrated that ten of its seventy-eight nation-clients in fiscal 1980 received more than half of the $11.5 billion in loan commitments. Most of these ten, moreover, exhibit a pattern of neglect of the needs and the rights of their poor majorities.

Take Indonesia, the bank's second-favorite client regime this year. According to the United Nation's International Labor Office, the nutritional status of Indonesia's poor worsens yearly. Yet what strikes foreign visitors to the central island of Java is the large number of luxury automobiles and fancy government edifices amid the squalor. President Suharto's regime squanders the nation's spectacular oil and gas revenues—$10 billion in 1980, almost the amount of total World Bank lending that year—on luxury imports, military hardware and showy, capital-intensive industrial projects that neither provide for the needs of Indonesia's majority nor generate desperately needed employment for the increasing numbers of jobless. And while the World Bank lends the Indonesian government up to $1 billion annually at very favorable interest rates, Indonesian oil revenues are being invested in the high-yielding Eurodollar markets.

Aiding Repressive Regimes

Moreover, at least three of the World Bank's top ten recipients—South Korea, the Philippines and Indonesia—are notorious for being among the most repressive governments in the world. Studies of the bank's loan allocations during the 1970s found a pattern of increased aid to countries that had undergone military takeovers or imposition of martial law. Uruguay, Chile, the Philippines and Argentina, for intance, received a sevenfold hike in bank lending during the 1970s at a time when bank loans overall had grown only threefold. Human-rights amendments to Congressional appropriations for the World Bank have not stopped a single loan to these regimes.

A public relations blitz by the World Bank has portrayed a major shift in its lending priorities from a "trickle-down," urban-based development strategy toward increased loans for "agriculture and rural development," "population, health and nutrition" and other activities trumpeted as providing opportunities and services to the poor. As bank vice president Hollis Chenery recently told *The New*

York Times, "The great bulk of recent World Bank lending has been to small farmers, through institutions at the grass roots." A quick scan of the bank's *Annual Report 1980,* however, reveals that little more than 30 percent of all money loaned came under the broadly defined heading of Agriculture and Rural Development and that fully 60 percent went to projects in the categories Power, Transportation, Industry, Development Finance, Telecommunications and Non-Project (i.e., direct financial support to governments).

Commitment to the Poor?

The World Bank's agriculture and rural development grants have been used as an instant measure of its commitment to the rural poor. But the overwhelming portion of funds allocated under this rubric do not go to so-called small farmers. Rather, they finance the construction of rural roads and electrification and irrigation projects—all of which benefit the better-off, commercially oriented farmers, merchants and landlords—as the bank's own evaluations of the programs have shown. Moreoever, a recently completed A.I.D. [Agency for International Development] survey of such "rural development" projects found that "operating and project expenditures for...rural-oriented activities are made primarily in the capital cities." The obvious result, the report concludes, is that "employment generated by these expenditures and their multipliers provides a significant incentive for rural-urban migration." Of course, few who flee landlessness and joblessness in the countryside find satisfactory work in the cities, especially as aid-generated jobs tend to go mostly to trained technicians, certified contractors and foreign consultants.

Sucking Away Individual Power

Our intervention via international financial institutions like the IMF and World Bank is much like our intervention through covert and overt military operations. Both kinds of "aid" strengthen central governments overseas without necessarily improving the *quality* of those governments. Both kinds of "aid" tend to concentrate power in existing leaders, and suck away what little power has been left in the hands of individuals, and in small businesses and living units.

Jonathan Kwitny, *Endless Enemies: The Making of an Unfriendly World,* 1984.

Another fundamental flaw undermines the World Bank's supposed poverty-oriented lending programs. Like the Bank of America,...the World Bank is primarily concerned with getting its loans repaid with interest; therefore, it can lend only to the "safe credit risks." In the Third World this means farmers who already control considerable farm assets and who can produce a sizable surplus for the market. Under such criteria, government agencies using World Bank financing will never help the truly small farmers, who till only a few acres as tenants, sharecroppers or subsistence growers. Yet these landless and near-landless people make up the majority of rural dwellers in at least twenty Asian and Latin American countries.

Thus, while the bank boasts of its small-farmer focus, nearly all of its farm lending actually goes to those with considerable land, market access and, above all, political clout. A World Bank rural credit project in the Philippines, for example, set aside 30 percent of its loan money for farmers with fewer than seventeen acres. Apart from the fact that most of the project funds still go to big operators, seventeen acres is hardly the appropriate cutoff point for defining a small farmer in the Philippines, where the average farm is only half that size.

Harmful Emphasis on Creditworthiness

The bank's emphasis on "creditworthiness" does more than simply bypass the world's rural poor. The larger farmers use their bank credit to expand their holdings and to apply new technologies to their farms. Land prices and rents soar, renters are evicted and machines take over the jobs of the landless laborers. The small-holders, who must depend on private moneylenders for credit at usurious rates, find it even harder to stay in business. They soon join the already swollen ranks of the landless.

Bolstering highly inequitable and repressive social structures in the Third World is only one of the accomplishments of the World Bank....As top-level policy makers point out every year to Congress, these programs are a tremendous boost to U.S.-based multinational corporations....Every dollar that U.S. taxpayers pay into the World Bank generates about $10 in procurement contracts for U.S. companies....As one lobbyist for the F.M.C. Corporation, a large international producer of machinery and chemicals, put it, "We don't see foreign aid as a liberal issue, we see it as part of world trade and we are part of world trade. Clearly, foreign aid is of interest to us."

Role of Foreign Aid

Foreign aid also has a critical role to play in the maintenance of highly inequitable global financial structures. Led by the nonoil-producing nations, which are hardest hit by rising interest rates and oil prices, the Third World now owes more than half a trillion dollars. The largest private banks, such as Citicorp and Bank of America, hold the notes for more than half of this debt, having outlent the public agencies by two-to-one during the last decade. Now, it seems, the private bankers are worried that they have overextended themselves in the unstable underdeveloped world. They want the World Bank and other "public" institutions such as the International Monetary Fund to supervise "austerity" measures that will insure timely repayment of their massive loans....

The closer integration of World Bank activities with private banking and direct multinational investments is evidenced by stepped-up discussions among high-level officials increased "cofinancing" of World Bank projects by private capital and about the expansion of the bank's International Finance Corporation, an agency that facilitates and participates in private-sector investments in the Third World....

Exploiting Less Developed Countries

[World Bank] loans will only increase the debts owed by the debt-ridden developing countries. Bolivia is already using 57 percent of its exports to pay off its loans, while Argentina is paying 52 percent of its imports and Brazil, 36.5 percent. Brazil owes the capitalist banks $101.8 billion; Mexico owes $95.9 billion. The developing countries' foreign debt rose from $200 billion in 1975 to $810 billion in 1984. The debt payments so far have all gone to pay part of the interest on the loans; they have not even touched the principal. It is estimated that every child born in these countries inherits a debt of $260—more than the per capita income in some of these countries.

How much more can the capitalist banks suck out of these countries?

The reason for the debt in the first place is the exploitation of the resources of the developing countries by the multinational corporations. The developing countries are a source of superprofits for the transnational banks and financial institutions.

"More Loans Are No Answer," *Daily World*, October 11, 1985.

Foreign economic aid programs, along with massive military aid and credit sales, export financing and investment insurance...serve to shore up the control of a relative few over the Third World's abundance of productive resources.

*"Governments do not come to the I.M.F. unless
their economies are in trouble, and the fund's
requirements are often the best medicine around."*

IMF Austerity Programs Are Essential for Stabilization

Henry S. Bienen and Mark Gersovitz

It is often said that the conditions the International Monetary Fund
sets for countries applying for loans are overly harsh, frequently
causing traumatic political turbulence. The authors of the following viewpoint, Henry S. Bienen and Mark Gersovitz, argue that the
austerity measures required by the IMF are necessary. Mr. Bienen
is professor of politics and international affairs at Princeton University. Mr. Gersovitz is a research economist there.

As you read, consider the following questions:

1. What alternatives do the authors see to the IMF's austerity
   requirements?
2. Why do the authors think that the IMF's requirements are
   better than the other alternatives?
3. What do the authors mean when they compare the IMF to
   "the messenger who carries the bad news"?

Henry S. Bienen and Mark Gersovitz, "I.M.F. Medicine," *The New York Times*, April 3,
1984. Copyright © 1984 by The New York Times Company. Reprinted by permission.

In the negotiations that led to the deal worked out to help Argentina meet the interest payments on its international debt, President Raúl Alfonsín cited concerns for his country's economic growth, stability and democracy. The deal may give Argentina some breathing space, but it does not answer lingering questions about how third world countries will service their debts. And in this, the International Monetary Fund deserves more credit than it usually gets.

The austerity conditions that the fund imposes on a developing country before agreeing to loan it money are often described as "bitter medicine." True, the magnitude of the required adjustments is often considerable, and conditions dictated to particular countries can be questioned. But governments do not come to the I.M.F. unless their economies are in trouble, and the fund's requirements are often the best medicine around.

Unfortunate Consequences

Certainly, economic programs imposed by the fund have occasionally had unfortunate political consequences. Devaluation triggered a military coup in Ghana in 1972, and the lifting of food subsidies has led, since 1977, to riots in Peru, Sierra Leone, Egypt, Liberia and the Sudan. But many countries operate year after year under I.M.F. conditions without serious political instability. Still others comply only partly with the fund's requirements, adjusting their policies to take account of domestic political repercussions. Nor does failing to reach agreement with the fund guarantee political stability: Michael Manley, former Prime Minister of Jamaica, who broke off negotiations with the fund, found he could not revive the economy and lost the 1980 elections.

What are the alternatives to an I.M.F. cure? One of the most common is the rationing of foreign exchange. This is meant to act as a tariff, helping the developing country to cut imports and replace them with goods produced at home. The problem is that such rationing usually gives a large bureaucracy discretion over coveted foreign currency, encouraging bribery and corruption among a few well-connected people. Inefficiencies in rationing mean that firms cannot get imported parts, industrial production is idled and people are thrown out of work. Often, the only groups that benefit are government managers, public-sector employees and capitalists who produce for the home market.

The other alternative for a strapped developing country is to refuse to service its international debt, raising the risk of eventual repudiation. No country has chosen this path for some time, but the possibility has ignited speculation about creditors' retaliatory weapons. Debtors may find that they can no longer transfer funds abroad or obtain trade credits. They may be reduced to cumbersome international barter. Others may find themselves unable to meet their bills with short-term borrowing and may have to depend

102

on their own savings for capital accumulation.

Some countries with large debts may feel that such isolation is a bearable price to pay for keeping the resources that would be used to service their debts. But many nations may be divided about this: Some groups within the country will prefer reaching agreement with the I.M.F., while others will feel that they would benefit from repudiation. Clearly, this would increase the prospects of political instability.

But economic stabilization programs are hardly the only—or even the most important—cause of political instability in the developing world. Argentina's military regime was deposed for political, not economic, reasons: It was discredited by the Falklands War and by popular anger at its repressive policies. Meanwhile, Chile's military regime has maintained control and even rallied some elements of the middle class despite the severe austerity measures it has imposed.

Promoting Meaningful Adjustment

Through the provision of temporary balance-of-payments financing, conditioned on the pursuit of appropriate macroeconomic policies, the IMF has served the dual purposes of promoting meaningful adjustment in individual countries and protecting the interests of the broader international community.

R.T. McNamar, in a speech, June 22, 1981.

In the Philippines, the assassination of opposition leader Benigno S. Aquino Jr. has had far more destabilizing effects than President Ferdinand E. Marcos's support for economic policies designed to meet I.M.F. conditions. And not even the repressive Marcos regime has been able to fully implement the fund's conditions: Repressing political opposition is not a necessary or sufficient condition for implementing coherent economic stabilization policies.

The relationship between political instability and the imposition of I.M.F. conditions is, at best, a tenuous one. A regime's human rights record, the reach of its bureaucracy, the style and competence of its leaders and the strength of the economic groups it must control—all will affect its ability to implement stabilization programs. Automatically blaming the I.M.F. for political instability in developing countries is merely blaming the messenger who carries the bad news.

> "To understand the political difficulties posed by
> the I.M.F.'s austerity programs, imagine how
> Americans would react if they were forced to
> comply with the Fund's strictures."

IMF Austerity Programs Cause Destabilization

Charles E. Schumer

Defenders of the International Monetary Fund's tough conditions
for countries wishing to obtain emergency loans often say that such
conditions are necessary to get the country back into a stable
economic condition. Charles E. Schumer, the author of the following viewpoint, disagrees. Mr. Schumer, a Democratic congressman
from New York and a member of the House Committee on Banking, Finance and Urban Affairs, writes that the IMF's requirements
are unrealistically harsh. He points out that "stable" countries such
as the US, which in 1985 had a trillion dollar federal deficit, would
never comply with such conditions and that, in fact, such austerity
requirements would lead to massive civil rebellion.

As you read, consider the following questions:

1. Why does the author believe that, theoretically, the US could
   be made subject to IMF requirements?
2. What does he think would be the political consequences if
   the US were subjected to such conditions?
3. What, in the opinion of the author, would be a good
   alternative to the present IMF requirements?

Today, in the midst of the worst international recession since the 1930's, many Latin American countries are having difficulty repaying bank loans. To prevent a default, the International Monetary Fund often intervenes, lending debtor nations some of the cash they need to make interest payments and, in return, insisting that they slash spending on social programs, abolish cost-of-living adjustments, raise taxes and restrict imports.

Not surprisingly, Latin American leaders are finding it politically difficult to implement the Fund's recommendations. As each day passes, political opposition increases and the potential for turmoil becomes more real. To understand the political difficulties posed by the I.M.F.'s austerity programs, imagine how Americans would react if they were forced to comply with the Fund's strictures.

Walk in Their Shoes

After one look at our $200 billion Federal deficit and $70 billion trade deficit, the Fund might well order Congress, the President and the Federal Reserve Board to slash spending on such social programs as food stamps, Medicaid and unemployment insurance; raise interest rates and taxes; abolish cost-of-living adjustments for military retirees, Social Security recipients and private-sector workers; and impose strict limits on the amount of foreign products Americans could purchase.

The Fund might also order the Fed to shrink the money supply and raise interest rates. As a result, automobile production and home-building would grind to a near halt, setting off a chain reaction of bankruptcies. The country's gross national product would plummet. Unemployment would rise to depression levels just as the Fund is forcing severe cuts in unemployment insurance, Medicaid, food stamps and every other safety-net program.

The International Monetary Fund would also demand an end to inflation indexing, thereby abrogating most union contracts with cost-of-living adjustments. Social Security recipients, military retirees, widows and orphans would be told to tighten their belts and allow inflation to reduce the real value of their benefits.

Severe Political Consequences

Complying with the Fund's demands for a balanced Federal budget would crack even President Reagan's "unshakeable commitment" to the I.M.F. Would the President sacrifice the MX missile, B-1 bomber and his plans for more nuclear aircraft carriers to the Fund's demands for a balanced Federal budget? And would he also allow the Fund to repeal the corporate and personal income tax cuts enacted just two years ago and then abort his plans to index personal income tax rates? Reaganomics, or at least large parts of it, would be in shambles.

The political consequences of adopting these policies so that the United States could continue paying interest to a consortium of foreign banks are not difficult to predict. Instead of allowing standards of living and the economy to be ground down, Americans would resist. Congressmen would denounce the I.M.F., arguing that default might be preferable to cutting so many programs. The President might announce that he would not allow the Fund to destroy his plans for economic renewal. And political leaders would comply with the Fund's policies only at the risk of their careers.

The United States is among the world's most stable democracies.

"General, you guarantee us that you can keep your peasants and workers quiet, and you can get all the IMF money you need."

Ollie Harrington for the *Daily World*.

Yet, if an I.M.F. austerity program could provoke turmoil here, imagine how it is undermining political stability in Brazil and Argentina.

To date, political leaders in Latin America have tried to implement the Fund's recommendations. They do not want to default. They know that their countries depend on bank loans for most of the capital they need for economic growth. Nevertheless, the prospect of several more years of austerity might push them over the brink. Already, political rumblings can be heard, and we may soon approach the time when political leaders decide that default or repudiation is the least painful option.

Aims of US Policy

The United States is now spending millions of dollars for military aid to prevent the overthrow of a few small Central American governments. Yet we are pursuing economic policies that could undermine the political stability of several of the largest countries in the hemisphere.

To prevent instability and to reduce the prospects of default, Congress should approve...a provision encouraging the Fund to adopt less austere policies, including stretching out debt repayments at lower interest rates.

Easing repayment terms will improve the chances that banks will be repaid and will promote political stability in Latin America. These are the proper aims of United States policy.

"The imperialist powers are deliberately dragging out a settlement of the [debt] problem in order to perpetuate the credit dependence, and with it the political dependence, of the Third World on the West."

The IMF Works Against National Interests

Mikhail Burlakov

Mikhail Burlakov, a writer for the Communist weekly *New Times*, believes that the International Monetary Fund is harming Third World countries more than it is helping them. In the following viewpoint, he states that in addition to making debts nearly impossible to pay, IMF policies force countries to accept capitalist values at the expense of their true national interests. Consequently, the less developed countries remain both economically and politically dependent on the large, imperialist countries.

As you read, consider the following questions:

1. Where does the author believe the root of the Third World debt problems lies?
2. The author argues that Third World countries have actually given the IMF and its imperialist sponsors more than it has received from them. What kind of proof does he offer for this claim?
3. According to the author, what connection is there between the US arms buildup and the Third World debt crisis?

Mikhail Burlakov, "The Debt Problem: Can It Be Resolved?" *New Times*, No. 41, October 1985.

For many Third World countries foreign credits, instead of being a stimulus to economic development, have become the main brake on their economies and principal cause of the impoverishment of their peoples. Credits extended to the Third World have in recent years become an instrument of neocolonialist plunder.

The International Monetary Fund and the big Western creditor banks lay the entire blame for the situation that has emerged on the developing countries which, they say, have borrowed too much, made insufficiently effective use of loans and ceased to control the growth of indebtedness. This supposedly is the cause of the present foreign debt crisis.

Unequal Economic Power

True enough, many developing countries lack the experience the Western industrial countries have in international currency and credit operations. However, the roots of the debt crisis lie in the unequal economic relations between these two groups of countries, the dependent status of the developing countries in the capitalist world economy and its monetary and financial system.

Credit extended in the guise of "development aid" has in recent years become one of the basic forms of the neocolonialist plunder of the Third World. The monetary and credit policy of the U.S. and the expansion of the banking monopolies have created a machinery for siphoning out financial and material resources and this makes it possible to shift the burden of the West's economic difficulties onto the shoulders of Third World countries. An integral part of this neocolonialist plunder are protectionist practices in relation to the developing countries and their involvement in the ruinous arms buildup. Thus, the responsibility for the debt crisis retarding the social and economic development of the Third World rests with the imperialist powers....

The IMF and the International Bank for Reconstruction and Development have latterly begun to speak of the debt problem having become less acute since the Western creditors have granted developing countries deferments on repayment of their debts. Actually, however, deferment of debts at high interest rates does not solve the problem, but merely puts off its solution. Meanwhile the debts continue to grow: in 1984 they increased by 6 per cent and a further growth of 8.5 per cent is expected this year.

According to [World Bank] data, last year the Third World paid the developed capitalist countries more than they received from it. Payments by the developing countries on principal and interest ran to $126.6 billion, while they received from the West only $85 billion in new credits, financial aid, and investments.

The economic recovery that set in last year in a number of Third World countries increased their average annual economic development rate by roughly 3 per cent. Nevertheless their foreign indebtedness is not declining. Experts estimate that it will increase from $895 billion to $1 trillion. Thus, even in a relatively favourable economic situation the growth rate of debts exceeds that of the economy of the debtor countries more than three times over....

Imposed War Preparations

The financial situation in Third World countries, especially in those with pro-Western regimes, is worsened also by the arms buildup imposed upon them by imperialism. Invoking a mythical "external threat" and artificially creating regional seats of tension, the NATO countries, in their search for bigger markets for their arms concerns, are inducing developing countries to buy costly armaments. As a result, the share of the Third World in the world's total military spending has increased from 4 to 16 per cent since the early sixties, and today it spends more than $100 billion on war preparations annually. The West's policy of whipping up international tension has led to a situation when the military spending of the developing countries is roughly equal to their payments on their foreign debts and interest on them.

Tool of Imperialism

The major characteristic of imperialism is the export of capital. In order to facilitate the movement of capital and promote international trade, the U.S., along with the other major imperialist countries, created the International Monetary Fund (IMF) and the International Bank for Reconstruction and Development (the World Bank)....

Today, the main role of the IMF is providing emergency loans to countries and acting as a loan approval agency for private banks. In many cases it uses those loans to further the U.S. policy of domination. For instance, a recent study commissioned by the Congressional Research Service found the U.S. frequently uses its influence with the IMF and the World Bank to "obtain or reject loans for countries based on how well it likes the policies of their governments." The study also reported that "the U.S. has a 'hit list' of countries it will prevent for political reasons from borrowing money from the IMF and other international financial institutions."

Daily World, April 9, 1985.

War preparations swallow up a larger share of the state budgets in many Third World countries than even in NATO countries. In Chile, for example, 32 per cent of budget expenditure goes for military purposes, in Paraguay 24 per cent, in Argentina 23.1 per cent, and in Egypt 15 per cent. In the poorest regions of the planet, where 95 per cent of the population is illiterate and where only one out of three has access to medical care, $268 million are spent every day for military purposes! The $100 billion the Third World spends for these purposes could pay, experts estimate, for 300 steam power stations of 120,000 kilowatt capacity each, 300 oil refineries, 1,000 chemical fertilizer works, 1,600 sugar refineries, 10,000 hospitals or 20 million flats. Such is the enormous economic and social price the developing world has to pay today for international tension.

Intolerable Situation

For many years now the economy of the Third World has been bled white by the pumping out to the Western countries of capital badly needed for economic development, the foreign exchange losses resulting from unfair trade practices, the depreciation of national currencies, the rising cost of living, and the arms buildup imposed by imperialism. In the eighties these economic disasters have been compounded by the foreign debt crisis, although actually it is not the developing countries that are in debt to the West, but the latter that owes the Third World more than it can ever pay.

In 1975-85 the developing countries paid Western creditors some $900 billion in principal and interest—a sum five times their foreign indebtedness in 1975 ($180 billion). Interest payments alone in the past five years have run to $235 billion, or more than the total debt of the Third World in 1975.

However, the debt that has already been repaid many times over continues to grow much faster than the debtor countries' ability to pay....

Forced Political Conditions

The Washington-controlled International Monetary Fund is forcing upon the debtor countries political and economic terms of repayment that often have no direct relation to their foreign debt commitments. In exchange for deferment of payment on old loans and for new credits they are expected to take drastic socio-economic measures which directly impinge on the living standard of broad sections of the population.

The so-called "stabilization programmes" imposed on Third World countries by the IMF prescribe the reduction of state appropriations for medical care, education and other social needs, wage cuts, devaluation of national currencies, and the ending of state food price subsidies. At the same time, the IMF presses the governments of the debtor countries to give foreign capital freer access to their economies and to dismantle the state sector, which is tantamount to eliminating the very foundations of economic independence. The austerity measures the IMF insists upon essentially disregard the external conditions for the settlement of the debt problem, although the reasons for the emergence and aggravation of the debt crisis lie precisely in the West's economic relations with the Third World....

The attempts made over the past three years to resolve the debt crisis by IMF and Washington prescriptions have demonstrated

The Growth of the Foreign Debt of the Developing Countries
(in billions of dollars)

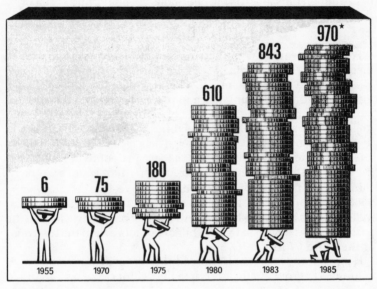

6	75	180	610	843	970*
1955	1970	1975	1980	1983	1985

*Forecast

New Times, October 1985.

that far from coping with the problem they are giving it dimensions that threaten the entire world economy. The imperialist powers are deliberately dragging out a settlement of the problem in order to perpetuate the credit dependence, and with it the political dependence, of the Third World on the West.

At their international forums within the framework of the non-aligned movement and at special conferences on the debt problem—held last year in Quito, Ecuador, and in Cartagena, Colombia—the developing countries went on record that the problem is not a purely economic one but requires a political solution. The leaders of many Third World countries hold that the way out of the critical situation should be sought in a comprehensive programme that would take into account both the external and internal factors of their economic development. Some elements of this programme have already been formulated and are supported by the majority of the debtor countries.

Top priority among international measures capable of substantially easing the economic straits of the developing countries belongs to the ending of the arms race unleashed by the West and the channelling of part of the resources thus released to development purposes. This position has been repeatedly set forth by Third World spokesmen at forums of the non-aligned movement and at U.N. General Assembly sessions. Many prominent leaders of the Third World hold that the safeguarding of international security and disarmament should be linked with the promotion of economic and social progress in the developing countries. The countries of the socialist community have on repeated occasions put forward concrete initiatives to this end.

It is common knowledge that the White House is financing the "rearmament of America" largely at the expense of other peoples. It has to be paid for also by the developing countries from where capital attracted by high bank rates flows to the U.S. Thus, the U.S. arms buildup policy is directly associated with its policy of costly international credit and the overrated dollar, which is sapping the world capitalist economy and the economy of the developing debtor countries. The need for a change in the destructive monetary and credit policy of the U.S. and other Western countries is logically associated by the developing countries with the broader issue of the need for the fundamental restructuring of the international monetary system now based on the hegemony of the dollar.

Strengthening the Developing Countries

The solution of the debt problem also presupposes the strengthening of the economic and foreign trade positions of the majority of the developing countries, which buy from 30 to 40 per cent of the exports of the industrial states. The newly independent states rightly urge that the West renounce its protectionist policy which artificially checks the growth of their exports and limits their ability to import goods and services from the developed countries. What is needed is a general liberalization of the terms of international trade that would make for its expansion, hasten the economic development of the Third World, and at the same time help to resolve its debt problem.

The debtor countries are also sharply critical of the very idea of "bilateral" negotiations on debts the Western creditors are insisting upon. Such "bilateral negotiations" are conducted with individual debtor countries by the IMF, which represents the interests of the U.S. and other Western creditor countries. The obvious inequality of the parties to such talks enables the IMF to compel each debtor country separately to accept its "stabilization programme" designed to ensure repayment of debts regardless of the national interests of the given country. In view of this, the developing countries consider it necessary to restructure the international trade and monetary and credit organizations in such a way as to ensure the observance of democratic procedures practised in U.N. agencies. A concrete step in this direction could be made in the course of global talks within the U.N. framework on a wide range of problems of trade, development and monetary and credit relations.

> *"The biggest beneficiaries of the I.M.F.'s policies are the multinational banks, whose reckless lending helped create the debt crisis in the first place."*

The IMF Works Against the Poor

Chuck Lane

Chuck Lane is a staff writer for *The New Republic*, a weekly opinion magazine. In the following viewpoint, he argues that the International Monetary Fund fails to achieve its purported goal of helping the world's poor. The IMF is, he claims, riddled with the values of conservative bankers. Consequently the goal of profit-making overrides the national interests of the countries to which it loans money.

As you read, consider the following questions:

1. According to the author, why do the leaders of less developed countries institute harsh economic measures even though they know these measures will increase the tensions and instabilities of their countries?
2. In what ways does the author believe that private banks benefit from the policies of the IMF?
3. What does the author view as the solution to the debt problems of less developed countries?

Chuck Lane, "Dunning Democracy," *The New Republic*, June 4, 1984. Reprinted by permission of THE NEW REPUBLIC, © 1984, The New Republic, Inc.

On April 19 [1984] Salvador Jorge Blanco, the President of the Dominican Republic, announced that he was devaluing the Dominican peso by 200 percent—a move which instantly doubled the prices Dominicans pay for imported necessities such as food, cooking oil, and medicine. The urban poor, already enduring 30 percent unemployment, were infuriated by this call for more belt tightening. They rioted in cities all over the island, and Blanco dispatched his army to quell the unrest. After three days, the troops had restored order, but at a terrible cost: sixty people were killed, and two hundred wounded. One hundred opposition leaders were later arrested. Independent radio stations are still under military control. The riots not only jolted President Blanco's government, they threatened the future of Dominican democracy itself, which was restored just six years ago after decades of dictatorial right-wing rule.

Why did Blanco institute such politically destructive measures? The International Monetary Fund demanded them. If he had refused, the fund would have withheld the next installment of the $400 million loan it negotiated with Blanco last year. The Dominican Republic is desperate for cash because the price of its main export, sugar, has dropped by over 20 percent in the last five years; now its $450 million annual oil import bill uses up two-thirds of its export earnings. The country's foreign exchange reserves are so low it is unable to repay its $2.6 billion foreign debt. The I.M.F. was the only source of credit it could find.

IMF Is "Ruler"

As the "lender of last resort" to Third World nations, the I.M.F. has acquired so much influence over these countries' finances that one former member of Peru's cabinet recently called it "the ruler of the developing world." Like most unelected rulers, it abuses its powers. In country after country, I.M.F. policies have done what they did in the Dominican Republic: hinder economic growth, foment political instability, and undermine democracy. The fund does its damage with the help of American tax dollars—and at the expense of American jobs—but the only Americans who benefit are the ones who happen to run multinational banks.

The I.M.F.'s current predatory role is nothing like what the Western industrial countries intended when they set up the I.M.F. at the 1944 economic summit in Bretton Woods, New Hampshire. The idea was that member nations would pay into the fund and then borrow foreign exchange from it during short-term balance-of-payments deficits. (The U.S. Treasury, and hence the U.S. taxpayer, made by far the largest contribution then, as it does today—$18.6 billion.) Everyone thought the fund's mission would remain relatively modest. But the 1973 OPEC price shock changed all that. Western banks "recycled" OPEC's huge dollar surpluses by lending billions to developing countries—on the assumption,

115

sometimes warranted, often not, that their economies would grow enough to ensure full repayment. Then came the 1975 recession. Prices for Third World exports fell, but oil import bills stayed high. The developing countries' reserves of hard currency all but vanished. The I.M.F. stepped into the breach, supplying enormous amounts of hard currency that the developing countries needed to make debt payments to the banks. And after the second oil price shock in 1979, and the recession that followed it in 1982, debtor countries became even more dependent on the I.M.F. Today some forty countries owe the fund a total of $32 billion.

Tough Strings Attached

But I.M.F. loans come with strings attached. The fund only lends to nations that agree to economic "adjustment" measures designed to rebuild their reserves of foreign exchange—and hence their capacity to pay off foreign debt. The I.M.F. requires governments to restrict imports and boost exports, usually by devaluing their currencies, cutting wages, and increasing taxes. These austerity steps halt economic growth and impose severe economic pain on the people of the debtor countries. (And they can mean starvation for the poorest of the poor, since many Third World countries import most of their food.) Yet usually debtor countries have no choice but to give in to the I.M.F. The banks regard acceptance of I.M.F. strictures as evidence of a country's creditworthiness—and won't supply credit to countries that reject them.

Perverted Agency for Bank

Although the IMF was designed 40 years ago as a currency stabilizer, it has been perverted into a collection agency for Western banks, an instrument of political repression and a source of social unrest in the developing world.

Robert Lekachman, *Los Angeles Times*, June 19, 1984.

Of course, imposing austerity on countries that already have large populations of poor people is a recipe for political unrest. When the protests begin, governments often have just two choices: political suicide, or repression. The I.M.F. thus encourages the worst tendencies of authoritarian rulers. In Brazil, for example, which is now in its second year of I.M.F. austerity, wage cuts and price hikes have sparked strikes and bread riots. The military government has responded by declaring martial law in some cities, and by postponing a long-promised return to free elections. And the fund makes life all but impossible for democrats. Salvador Jorge Blanco only preserved his government in the Dominican Republic by taking uncharacteristically repressive measures. The Nigerian military had many reasons for overthrowing the democratic government of

President Shehu Shagari last January; the last straw was his austerity budget designed, in part, to appease the I.M.F. President Fernando Belaunde Terry of Peru is currently being pressured by the I.M.F. to raise taxes and food prices—at a time when Peruvian democracy already faces a double political threat from a major recession and Maoist "Shining Path" guerrillas.

Banks Are Beneficiaries

The biggest beneficiaries of the I.M.F.'s policies are the multi-national banks, whose reckless lending helped create the debt crisis in the first place. The I.M.F. shields them from the consequences of their own shortsightedness, making sure that debt payments continue to be made, and that the banks can therefore keep showing profits on their quarterly balance sheets. Take the Dominican case. The currency devaluation will reduce the country's imports and cheapen its exports. Dollars that Dominicans used to pay to U.S. food producers will remain in the country; more dollars will flow in to pay for Dominican products. But the money won't stay on the island; it will go straight to the banks that hold the Dominican Republic's $2.6 billion foreign debt. The $400 million loan from the I.M.F.—which came courtesy of American taxpayers—will end up on Wall Street, too. The Dominican Central Bank will use it to pay interest.

So, just as the I.M.F. redistributes money from the Third World to the United States, it also helps American financiers at the expense of American manufacturers and workers. Forcing debtor countries to cut imports and send every dollar they can scrape up to the bankers wrecks America's overseas markets. According to a story by Everett G. Martin in the *Wall Street Journal*, austerity measures cut the imports of Latin American countries by $30 billion between 1981 and 1983. This reduced the Latin American sales of U.S. companies by $16.3 billion. Martin estimated that this caused a net loss of more than 400,000 American jobs....

Need for Reform

The I.M.F. doesn't need to be scrapped or replaced, just reformed. It should help banks do for debtor countries what banks already do for corporate customers who have trouble paying their debt: set up "work-out" arrangements which extend repayment schedules and provide new credit at reduced interest rates. Congress endorsed the work-out approach in an amendment to the Reagan Administration's bill increasing the American contribution to the I.M.F. by $8.4 billion. The amendment, drafted by Democratic Representative Charles Schumer, requires the U.S. members of the I.M.F. board—who have an effective veto over I.M.F. policy decisions—to vote down adjustment programs where the banks involved refuse to offer the debtor country new long-term loans at low interest. The law applies to every country whose annual foreign debt payments are more than 85 percent of its foreign exchange earnings. Developing countries would still have to pay their debts. But by reducing interest payments, work-outs reduce the need for I.M.F.-imposed austerity. This would leave debtor countries with more money to rebuild their economies and buy American goods. Best of all, it would break the dangerous cycle of unrest and repression which chokes off the development of democratic governments.

Usurers' "Cash Cow"

The banks have accommodated themselves to the prospect of not being repaid by charging what used to be considered usurous rates. One bank official was recently quoted as saying, "We hope they [an unnamed major borrower] never pay us back. They are a cash cow for us." Like other usurers, the interest is the main attraction and the banks hope it goes on forever. So much for altruism and the public interest.

Tom Corcoran, *USA Today*, May 1984.

The banks, of course, have resisted the work-out idea, because it would make them take what bankers call an "earnings hit" in the short run—that is, it would reduce quarterly profits. But that's only fair, considering how much the banks did to create the debt crisis. In any case, work-outs would help the banks in the long run. Much of the interest money the banks are getting now from debtor countries comes from short-term, high-interest loans which the banks themselves provided. The banks count on the I.M.F. to enforce austerity and squeeze out the dollars needed to pay this mounting high-interest debt. But one day a large, relatively self-sufficient debtor like Brazil or Argentina may decide that it's had enough austerity and repudiate the I.M.F., leaving the banks with far more bad debt to write off than they would ever have under a work-out.

> *"IMF stabilization programs assume that the problems that led to instability result from bad domestic policies....But these are not the main causes."*

The IMF Works Against Economic Realities

Michael Moffitt

Michael Moffitt is an investment advisor at Shearson/American Express in New York and an associate fellow at the Institute for Policy Studies in Washington, DC. In the following viewpoint, he contends that the International Monetary Fund too frequently fails at its stated goals. Instead of stabilizing the economies of less developed countries and restoring the balance of payments on their debts, IMF policies cause economic and social disaster. Incorrectly assessing the nature of national debt problems, the IMF prescribes the wrong solutions.

As you read, consider the following questions:

1. According to the author, what specific kinds of social and economic disaster occur as a result of IMF policies?
2. Does the author believe that failures of IMF programs are entirely the IMF's fault?
3. What, in the opinion of the author, is the basic incorrect assumption that the IMF bases its policies on?

Michael Moffitt, *The World's Money*. New York: Simon & Schuster, 1983. Copyright © 1983 by Michael Moffitt. Reprinted by permission of SIMON & SCHUSTER, Inc.

In theory, IMF officials sit down with government ministers to work out solutions to a country's economic problems. In reality the relationship is inevitably adversarial, and the country's bargaining power is limited by the knowledge that if it does not accept the IMF's conditions, it will be closed out of world credit markets. Basically, the Fund lays down a series of conditions, spelled out in what is known as a standby arrangement, which the country agrees to meet before it gets IMF money....When a country violates the performance criteria, the IMF tears up the agreement. Generally the finance minister is sacked and frequently the government falls.

IMF economic "stabilization" programs have traditionally been austere. Like the old gold standard, they emphasize cutting government spending, devaluing the currency, increasing unemployment and raising interest rates in order to restore financial integrity. Essentially what the Fund does to a country in trouble is administer a tough, quick-fix solution to its balance of payments problems. The IMF, which does not consider itself a development institution, is less concerned with solving the structural dilemmas of development than with generating a quick improvement in a country's balance of payments....

IMF Strategy

What the Fund strategy boils down to is making radical cuts in domestic consumption in order to free up resources to service the foreign debt. Wages must fall dramatically in real terms in hopes that exports will become more competitive. Simultaneously, currency devaluation and lifting price controls pushes up prices beyond the reach of many consumers. Imports will decline and new production will be diverted to the export market. The hope of the IMF technocrats is that rising exports and falling imports will lead to "equilibrium" in the balance of payments, thereby restoring creditworthiness. If it does, the IMF then leans on the banks to contribute more money as a reward for being successful. Occasionally, for important Western allies, such as Turkey, Pakistan or Seaga's Jamaica, the United States and western Europe assemble massive supplementary financing that makes the IMF medicine easier to swallow.

In poor countries IMF programs typically bring economic and social disaster. When a country reduces domestic consumption to free up resources to pay off its creditors, somebody else must get less. When the IMF and the banks get together to "solve" a Third World country's foreign debt problems, the usual losers are the urban workers and the rural poor. Devaluing the currency and abolishing price controls on food and other necessities sends the cost of living skyward, so the majority of the population is forced to spend most of its income just to survive. Cuts in government spending inevitably lead to recession, increasing unemployment and lowering wages. (The IMF often reasons that when food prices go up, poor farmers will be among the main beneficiaries. Yet, even if food prices rise, the increasing costs of fuels, fertilizers and credit are often sufficient to render the impact of higher food prices negligible.) Meanwhile, the incomes of the rich go up—by design. The rich, according to conventional economic theory, are society's principal savers. Since it is out of savings that the funds for investment come, particularly if foreign borrowing is curtailed, the rich must be encouraged to save more so they can invest more. The IMF has never come up with a satisfactory solution of what to do if the rich put their additional income in Swiss banks or use it to buy real estate in Paris or Manhattan.

Wrong Economic Medicine

IMF austerity measures...often unnecessarily limit growth in the years ahead for both developing countries and the developed nations that deal with them (the developing world buys 40 percent of all U.S. exports). If the developing countries follow IMF prescriptions, the result will be more misery, the reason being that the fund is applying the wrong economic medicine. Most of the developing world's debt is the result of external variables—the most important of which is the U.S. monetary policy—not excess demand. But the fund is too caught in its deflationary world to see the difference.

And there is a difference. Most nations' problems are deep-rooted and not simply the result of profligate behavior. By tightening the credit supply to get at inflation, the Federal Reserve reduced inflation. But the deep worldwide recession that followed, combined with the rise in the price of oil in 1979, has devastated the economies of many countries—developing countries in particular. Debt has become a way of life for these nations, so much so that the short-term austerity programs offered by the fund are not achieving the structural adjustment that is needed. The only way to alleviate the externally induced pain is to become less reliant on it—to substitute domestic for foreign-produced goods. Unfortunately for these countries—and for the world—the fund has been content simply to hack away at inflation and resist providing incentives for growth.

John Eisendrath, *The Washington Monthly*, February 1983.

The injustices of IMF programs have led to food riots in Lima, Cairo, Kinshasa and Rabat. The political fallout from IMF programs has toppled governments in Turkey and Jamaica. In 1977, the rigors of the IMF's approach nearly brought down the government of Anwar Sadat. The governments that have survived a dose of IMF economics frequently are military governments. In Turkey the overthrow of democracy by the military in 1980 was a direct result of an IMF stabilization program. The IMF, one observer told the *New York Times*, "has overthrown more governments than Marx and Lenin combined.''

Despite the costs of the IMF's policies, countries might not be so reluctant to submit to the Fund's shock treatment if the programs had a reasonably successful track record. That they do not is confirmed by the Fund's own staff. According to an analysis performed by T. R. Reichmann, an economist in the Fund's powerful Trade and Exchange Relations Department, 21 stabilization programs initiated after Oil Shock I had only about a 33 percent success rate. The mixed results of more recent Fund programs were described candidly in a speech by IMF Managing Director Jacques de Larosiere. In a survey of 23 programs implemented in 1978 and 1979, according to Larosiere, only half of them could be considered successes. Moreover, the success stories tended to be concentrated in lesser developed European economies such as Turkey and Portugal, not in the poor countries of Asia, Africa, Latin America and the Caribbean. In only half the cases did the programs reduce external deficits and inflation in line with the targets established by the Fund. While the 50 percent success rate is an improvement over the results of the early 1970s, the dilemma facing a government with massive debt problems is whether the costs of the Fund's approach can be justified by the benefits.

In fairness to the Fund, not all of this is due to its own shortcomings. One of the reasons why the Fund is forced to rely on quick-fix programs is its lack of resources, which are minuscule compared to the balance of payments problems with which it is supposed to cope. Only the massive debt crises in Mexico and Brazil prompted the Reagan administration to drop its outspoken opposition to a major increase in the IMF's resources. The major industrialized countries are now preparing to approximately double the Fund's $60 billion in resources to shore up a badly strained banking system.

Basic Flaw

Yet no amount of money can compensate for the basic flaw of the IMF's approach to the economic problems of Third World countries. No three-year economic program can remedy problems that have been decades or even centuries in the making. IMF stabilization programs assume that the problems that led to instability result from bad domestic policies. To be sure, inefficiencies, corruption and rotten governments abound. But these are not the main causes of the massive balance of payments problems of the 1970s and early 1980s. The principal causes remain the structural dilemmas of development and global economic fluctuations over which Third World countries have little influence. The most immediate example of this is the dramatic increase in world oil prices in the 1970s. Oil is an essential raw material in the industrialization process. For countries that do not have oil, no amount of tinkering with domestic monetary policy can make OPEC price increases easier to swallow.

The IMF bases its faith in monetary manipulation largely on the experience of the industrial economies. In these countries, technological prowess plus tremendous financial resources make it possible to design macroeconomic policies that allow them to cope with severe dislocations such as oil price increases. In the Third World, short-run macroeconomic policies are often secondary to the real economic problems characteristic of underdevelopment. In a speech to the 1980 IMF annual meeting, Amir Jamal, the finance minister of Tanzania, put it this way:

> If in an industrial economy a boiler explodes, the results are of a purely micro nature, and anyhow, it can probably be replaced in 48 hours. With us, it can be very different. If the boiler of a large, remote coffee curing works explodes, it may take 48 weeks to obtain a replacement. And in the meantime, the effects on overall exports, government revenue and bank borrowing, as well as storage capacity, are significant at a macro as well as a micro level. I very much doubt that indicators and targets related to cyclical demand management within industrial economies are the best yardsticks for measuring these realities....Added to this is a wholly unrealistic time-frame quite unrelated to time for recovery from external bettering of achievement of real adjustments in production. These factors, plus the imponderables which make any single figure projection arbitrary, make of "conditionality" either a procrustean bed or a carte blanche for further Fund policy prescriptions.

In short, grinding down an economy to restore temporary equilibrium in the balance of payments not only imposes undue hardship on the population, it may be irrelevant to the real problems at hand.

Distinguishing Bias from Reason

When dealing with highly controversial subjects, many often will allow their feelings to dominate their powers of reason. Thus, one of the most important critical thinking skills is the ability to distinguish between statements based upon emotion and those based upon a rational consideration of the facts.

Most of the following statements are taken from the viewpoints in this chapter. Consider each statement carefully. *Mark R for any statement you believe is based on reason or a rational consideration of the facts. Mark B for any statement you believe is based on bias, prejudice, or emotion. Mark I for any statement you think is impossible to judge.*

If you are doing this activity as a member of a class or group, compare your answers with those of other class or group members. Be able to explain your answers. You may discover that others will come to different conclusions than you. Listening to the reasons others present for their answers may give you valuable insights in distinguishing between bias and reason.

If you are reading this book alone, ask others if they agree with your answers. You will find this interaction very valuable.

> R = *a statement based upon reason*
> B = *a statement based upon bias*
> I = *a statement impossible to judge*

1. Credits extended to the Third World have become an instrument of neocolonialist plunder.
2. The International Monetary Fund, like most unelected rulers, abuses its powers.
3. Many developing countries lack the experience the Western industrial countries have in credit operations.
4. The economy of the Third World has been bled white by the Western countries.
5. The developing countries understandably want to restructure the international credit organizations to ensure democratic procedures.
6. In theory, IMF officials sit down with government ministers to work out solutions to a country's economic problems.
7. It is common knowledge that the White House is financing the "re-armament of America" at the expense of other peoples.
8. The developing world has to pay an enormous economic and social price for international tension.
9. If a country reduces its domestic consumption to pay off its creditors, someone in that country will have to receive less of that country's resources.
10. IMF loans come with strings attached.
11. The IMF relies more on quick-fix programs because of its lack of resources.
12. After the second oil price shock, debtor countries became more dependent on the IMF.
13. Because the World Bank is an international organization, its decisions affect the lives of millions.
14. The IMF encourages the worst tendencies of authoritarian rulers.
15. The multinational banks' reckless lending helped create the debt crisis in the first place.
16. One of the Bank's goals is to ease the painful existence of the world's poor.
17. The World Bank has been enormously successful.
18. The World Bank's aid goes to governments, not people, let alone the poor.

Bibliography

The following list of books, periodicals, and pamphlets deals with the subject matter of this chapter.

Tamir Agmon, Robert G. Hawkins, and Richard M. Levich, eds. — *The Future of the International Monetary System*. Lexington, MA: Lexington Books/DC Heath & Company, 1984.

Robert Z. Ailber — *The International Money Game*. New York: Basic Books, 1983.

James Bovard — "Behind the Words at the World Bank," *The Wall Street Journal*, September 30, 1985.

Business Week — "The IMF's Dilemma on World Debt Gets Worse," July 25, 1983.

A.W. Clausen — "Third World Debt and Global Recovery," *Vital Speeches of the Day*, April 1, 1983.

Darrell Delamaide — *Debt Shock: The Full Story of the World Credit Crisis*. Garden City, NY: Doubleday & Company, 1984.

Steve Ellner — "Subversion, IMF-Style," *Commonweal*, February 24, 1984.

Charles Maeschling Jr. — "The Credit Collapse," *Foreign Service Journal*, April 1983.

Blanca Reimer and Michael R. Sesit — "The IMF Is Less and Less Able to Stop the Bleeding," *Business Week*, October 10, 1983.

Susan Riley — "The World's Bankers Look to a Perilous Future," *Maclean's*, September 13, 1982.

Jeffrey Sacks — "How to Save the Third World," *The New Republic*, October 28, 1985.

Stephan Schwartzman — "Banking on Disaster," *Multinational Monitor*, June 15, 1985.

Kenneth S. Smith — "World Bank, IMF—Do They Help or Hurt the Third Word?" *U.S. News & World Report*, April 29, 1985.

Catharine Watson and Teresa Hayter — *Aid: Rhetoric and Reality*. London: Sydney Pluto Press, 1985.

James H. Wolfe — "The World Bank and Quiet Diplomacy," *USA Today*, September 1985.

4 CHAPTER

World Government

Internationalism

Introduction

H.G. Wells, in an article for the *Tribune*, London, wrote that "human history becomes more and more a race between education and catastrophe." An historian and writer of fiction, Wells was a passionate advocate of world government. He believed that the catastrophe of which he wrote could be averted only when all nations agreed that international conciliation take precedence over nationalistic ambitions.

There is alluring logic to the thinking of Wells and other proponents of world government. A world that is at one cannot make war upon itself: To do so would seem a contradiction in terms. Yet to some, world government is not the seductive panacea portrayed by many of its supporters. Indeed, while one group of opponents simply labels it a quixotic, unworkable dream, others see it as a far more dangerous and volatile alternative to the nation-state system. The viewpoints in the following chapter attempt to present some of the more prevalent arguments for and against world government.

"[World Government] is the best form of life possible for mankind."

World Government Is a Necessity

W. Warren Wagar

A Fulbright Scholar and a Ph.D. from Yale University, W. Warren Wagar has written and researched extensively on the subject of world government. His works include *The City of Man, Building the City of Man,* and *H.G. Wells and the World State.* In the following viewpoint, Mr. Wagar claims that world civilization is at a frightening crossroad. He argues eloquently that the only way to avoid annihilation is for humanity to accept and pursue the path of oneness through world government.

As you read, consider the following questions:

1. Why does Karl Jaspers suggest that no extraterrestrial life has made contact with us?
2. Why does the author feel that this is a key time during which to build a world civilization?
3. What do you think Alfred North Whitehead meant by: "The pure conservative is fighting against the essence of the universe"?

Warren Wagar, *The City of Man,* Boston: Houghton Mifflin Company, 1963. Copyright © 1963 by Warren Wagar. Reprinted by permission of Houghton Mifflin Company.

All through history, men have responded to the collapse of old social orders by creating new social orders extensive enough to secure civil peace and humane values within the geographical limits of the society. In the present crisis, since here on earth geographical limits no longer exist, the only possible response true to man's nature as a social animal, is the building of a world civilization. If the response has succeeded before, on a continental scale, it can succeed again, on a planetary scale. Nothing at least absolutely vetoes it. The remedy must be as efficacious as ever.

A word of explanation. An organic world civilization is not a Utopia....It will be a world of finite men and women, no less corruptible than the men and women of imperial Rome, the Han and Gupta empires, or medieval Latin Christendom. It will draw deeply on the durable wisdom of the traditional civilizations, and it will share in their human shortcomings. But it must be a flourishing concern, a business in full operation, able to minister to the needs of all men, able to respond flexibly to new crises, able to grow and thrive in growing. It is the best form of life possible for mankind in an age of unlimited technics [technology] and a world community of peril. Its contours can only be guessed at, and yet it will not arrive by accident. In some never exactly foreseeable measure, to anticipate the future is to bring it under control.

Time Is Growing Short

But we have long since passed the time when manly faith and simple courage in any quantity however great could guarantee us success. Because civilization-building takes centuries, and we may have only a few years left, it would be absurd to promise ourselves a happy ending in the tradition of fairy tales and celluloid melodramas. The wolves are not howling outside the ramparts of civilization: they have broken in. Their breath is hot on our cheeks. The human race has abruptly reached that unexpectedly dangerous stage in its evolution when it must live, and go on living for all time, with material means ready at hand to accomplish quickly and easily its total destruction. These material means will continue to increase in potency with each passing year. But the human beings who inherit this arsenal of ultimate weapons—biological, chemical, thermonuclear, radiological—will be in substance the same irritable apes who first overran the planet only a few thousand years ago. They may grow in knowledge and strength, but they cannot entirely escape their instincts. Can men, remaining men, always through bluff or diplomacy or good sense somehow manage to avoid Armageddon? Karl Jaspers suggests that perhaps no extraterrestrial species has made contact with ours for the precise reason that no race can survive anywhere in the cosmos which has reached man's present level of technology. They all annihilate themselves in thermonuclear holocausts. And Jaspers, though hopeful, admits that our survival is intellectually "improbable." In brief, we are guilty and doomed to die unless we can escape to the sanity of a new civilization built to the world scale of human intercourse....

Posterity Demands It

Whoever enlists in the cause of man in this age will find no time for nostalgia. We are the link between the traditional civilizations of a well remembered past and the emergent world civilization. We stand between. If we break under the strain, there will be no future. All posterity is in our keeping. Such a task against such towering

---

An Affirmation of Human Oneness

I am a member of the Family of Man.
My home is Earth.
The achievements of Mankind
throughout the ages are my heritage.
My destiny is bound to that of all my
fellow Human Beings.
What we jointly create forms
our bequest to future generations.
Let me do no harm to my Family.
Let us not do harm to those yet to come.

World Federalists Association.

---

odds joins man to man and weaves meaning into the vast fabric of confusion. It can be the difference between the life and death of the soul....

The dream of an integrated world order is one of the oldest rational visions of civilized man. In a sense, it created civilization. Yet the dream has never been fully translated into reality, even in the largest empires. Premodern men lacked the physical means, and would-be integrators time and again suppressed ways of life and habits of thought unlike their own, preferring the whips of compulsion to the arts of integration, when they were put to the test. In theory and practice both, man has never been one psychospiritually organic species. He has wanted to be, and his human finitude has defeated him. Every quest for one God, one ultimate Reality, one brotherhood of man, one true faith, and one true commonwealth is a search, against the grain of man's egoism, for world order; but he captures an authentic vision of his goal only rarely, like a mountain peak glimpsed for a moment through heavy clouds....

As Alfred North Whitehead once wrote, "Adventure or Decadence are the only choices offered to mankind. The pure conservative is fighting against the essence of the universe." So, for that matter, is the pure liberal, who would build only on foundations

Atomic cloud over Nagasaki, 20 minutes after blast on August 10, 1945.
United Press International, Inc.

of open air and boundless freedom. The new world order, and the cosmic order after that, will trace their descent back by an unbroken chain of minds to the earliest civilizations of man, and ultimately to the One God in whom we all have our being. Nothing human is from nothing; and nothing human is forever. But our emphasis must properly fall on the future, in a prophetic book. Into this future we send our sons, and from it, in man's relentless flight through time, they will never return.

"It seems to me that the advocates of world government do not understand the [international] political situation."

World Government Is a Fantasy

Walter Berns

A noted educator and writer, Walter Berns received his Ph.D. from the University of Chicago in 1950. He has taught at Louisiana University and Cornell University, where he was chairman of the Department of Government from 1963 to 1968. He has authored several books including *Freedom, Virtue, and the First Amendment* and *Constitutional Cases in American Government*. In the following viewpoint, Mr. Berns outlines what he believes would be some of the principal obstacles to a workable world government.

As you read, consider the following questions:

1. How does the author cite the United World Federalists as an example of the impossibility of world government?
2. How do US and Soviet differences complicate the possibility of a world government?
3. Why does the author think that world despotism would result from world government?

Walter Berns, "The Fantasy of World Government," *National Review*, April 22, 1961. Reprinted with permission from *National Review*, 150 East 35th St., New York, NY 10016.

It seems to me that the devotees of world government have minimized the difficulties involved; yet the experience of one of the major organizations devoted to the cause, the United World Federalists, points up these difficulties in a dramatic fashion. The members of the organization met and agreed, as one of them later reported, that "a global government able to enforce law (in the sense of 'domestic law') on individual violators was necessary... and...possible...(and) that the only practicable form for such a world government was the federal form." But the members disagreed sharply on how to bring the world federation about, how to name the founding members, how to delegate powers to it. The members became "enraged," accused each other of "political immaturity," and demanded that the charters of affiliated groups be revoked. Finally, a deep schism left the parent organization with only half of its membership. The group that sought to unite the world could not even remain united itself.

A Complex Political Problem

How, then, can we get world government?

This, of course, is a political problem. The Soviet Union does not trust the West; the West, I hope, does not trust the Soviet Union. Whatever the chances of reaching agreement on some aspect of atomic disarmament, neither is likely to submit to a world government controlled by the other. Neither is likely to submit to a government controlled by others, if such a thing were possible, without the right to nullify decisions taken by these others. The example of the veto in the Security Council allows us to be as certain of this as we have to be. But the right to nullify decisions taken in important matters is incompatible with government.

Thus, the advocates of world government must explain how they intend to get the consent of the Soviet Union; for, even if the West believed in the necessity of world government, the political situation would be determined by the existence of a powerful Communist Russia rigidly controlled by a Central Committee that appears unlikely to agree to any non-Communist world government. There are two paths to consent: persuasion and force. The devotees of world government must get the consent of the Soviet Union by persuasion, but this seems impossible; or by force, which means, in the present state of armaments, by atomic war. But it is atomic war that we are trying to avoid!

It seems to me that the advocates of world government do not understand the political situation. To say, as Robert M. Hutchins does, that "men will fight until they get their rights," is to lose sight of the fact that men have also fought to get more than their rights, and, furthermore, overlooks the fact that men sometimes have peculiar notions as to their rights. Less than any generation in the history of the West can we deny that there are sometimes madmen in power who are willing to commit any crime at any cost, even at a cost involving the lives of millions of people, in the name of an unjust cause, which they, in their madness, call their rights.

The conclusion is this: we cannot persuade the Soviets to join a non-Communist world government; we cannot force them to join by any method short of atomic war; there can be no world government without them.

The Bomb and World Despotism

The usual objection to this analysis is that whatever the disagreements separating the United States and the Soviet Union, they are insignificant beside the massive agreement that there must be no atomic war. The threat of the bomb compels this agreement, and the agreement is the required foundation of world government. According to one of the world federalists, "the argument for world government is simple and irrefutable."

World Government and Tyranny

The character of a world government, represented today in essence by the United Nations is reactionary—a return to absolutism and totalitarianism so abhorred by those who for generations have fled from the tyrannical governments of the Old World. There is nothing to check the absolute power of world government, its decrees, its judgments; its legislative acts are final.

Mrs. Wilson K. Barnes, National Society, Daughters of the American Revolution, April 18, 1961.

It is indeed simple, but it is not irrefutable. If the only agreement is the fear of atomic annihilation, the first concern of the world government must be to guard against the bomb. All the existing bombs, or at least all that are *supposed* to exist, will have been turned over to the World State to be guarded, somehow, someplace, by a mixed force of political janissaries—probably Swedes and Indians. But everyone will agree that this is not enough: it will also be necessary to guard against the future production of the bomb. This will require a police force, with the power to inspect everywhere at any time, and without a warrant. Its purpose will be to prevent the manufacture of the bomb and to ferret out potential manufacturers of the bomb—that is, anyone against whom there is the slightest suspicion. This will require eternal vigilance and rigorous methods. No world parliament can be allowed to filibuster while an accusation stands against one of the member states; it cannot be allowed in any way to stand against the swift intervention of the police force. The World Parliament would probably become the equivalent of the impotent Supreme Soviet; the head of the police force would probably have to intervene in the Parliament,

135

shouting, as Cromwell did in another parliament, "Come, come, I will put an end to your prating." In short, world government based only on the fear of the bomb will be world despotism.

The Greater of Two Evils

Even if we concede for a moment that this description of the world state is imaginary, we cannot, it seems to me, deny that it is possible. The question is, How *probable* is worldwide despotism? It seems especially probable if the threat of universal destruction is regarded as a greater evil than universal despotism, for this means that those who advocate world government will accept despotism in order to avoid destruction and, perhaps, even the threat of destruction. One is permitted to wonder whether that simple insight to which civilization is indebted—that there are greater evils than death and that there are some things for which men will give their lives—yet survives in modern man. Even we ought to know, as others knew 2,500 years ago, that fear is the principle of tyranny.

"A World Government is preferable to the far greater evil of wars."

World Government Could Bring Peace

Albert Einstein

Albert Einstein was a native of Germany. He is best known for his theory of relativity, for which he won the Nobel Prize for physics in 1921. A lifelong pacifist and advocate of internationalism, he was the author of *Why War?* (a correspondence with Sigmund Freud) and *The World as I See It*. In the following viewpoint, Dr. Einstein claims that the existence of the atomic bomb has made the need for world peace absolutely imperative and that world government may well be humanity's sole path to peace.

As you read, consider the following questions:

1. Why does Einstein suggest that Russia be invited to write the first draft of a world government constitution?
2. Why does Einstein recommend that the three great powers, united in a world government, have the right to intervene in the internal affairs of smaller countries?
3. Einstein does not see the minority government in Russia as a threat to world peace. What is his reasoning?
4. How does Einstein respond to the charge that world government could lead to world tyranny?

The release of atomic energy has not created a new problem. It has merely made more urgent the necessity of solving an existing one. One could say that it has affected us quantitatively, not qualitatively. As long as there are sovereign nations possessing great power, war is inevitable. That statement is not an attempt to say when war will come, but only that it is sure to come. That fact was true before the atomic bomb was made. What has been changed is the destructiveness of war.

I do not believe that civilization will be wiped out in a war fought with the atomic bomb. Perhaps two thirds of the people of the earth might be killed, but enough men capable of thinking, and enough books, would be left to start again, and civilization could be restored.

I do not believe that the secret of the bomb should be given to the United Nations organization. I do not believe that it should be given to the Soviet Union. Either course would be like the action of a man with capital, who, wishing another man to work with him on some enterprise, should start out by simply giving his prospective partner half of his money. The second man might choose to start a rival enterprise, when what was wanted was his cooperation.

Big Power Collaboration

The secret of the bomb should be committed to a World Government, and the United States should immediately announce its readiness to give it to a World Government. This government should be founded by the United States, the Soviet Union, and Great Britain—the only three powers with great military strength. All three of them should commit to this World Government all of their military strength. The fact that there are only three nations with great military power should make it easier rather than harder to establish such a government.

Since the United States and Great Britain have the secret of the atomic bomb and the Soviet Union does not, they should invite the Soviet Union to prepare and present the first draft of a Constitution for the proposed World Government. That action should help to dispel the distrust which the Russians already feel because the bomb is being kept a secret, chiefly to prevent their having it. Obviously the first draft would not be the final one, but the Russians should be made to feel that the World Government would assure them their security.

It would be wise if this Constitution were to be negotiated by a single American, a single Britisher, and a single Russian. They would have to have advisers, but these advisers should only advise when asked. I believe three men can succeed in writing a workable Constitution acceptable to all three nations. Six or seven men, or more, probably would fail.

After the three great powers have drafted a Constitution and adopted it, the smaller nations should be invited to join the World Government. They should be free to stay out; and though they would be perfectly secure in staying out, I am sure they would wish

'NOW, NOW! DON'T PANIC! AFTER I HAPPEN YOU WON'T FEEL A THING!'

Reprinted with permission from the *Minneapolis Tribune*.

to join. Naturally they should be entitled to propose changes in the Constitution as drafted by the Big Three. But the Big Three should go ahead and organize the World Government whether the smaller nations join or not.

The World Government would have power over all military matters and need have only one further power: the power to intervene in countries where a minority is oppressing a majority and creating the kind of instability that leads to war. Conditions such as exist in Argentina and Spain should be dealt with. There must be an end to the concept of non-intervention, for to end it is part of keeping the peace.

The Lesser of Two Evils

The establishment of the World Government must not have to wait until the same conditions of freedom are to be found in all three of the great powers. While it is true that in the Soviet Union the minority rules, I do not consider the internal conditions there are of themselves a threat to world peace. One must bear in mind that the people in Russia did not have a long political education, and changes to improve Russian conditions had to be carried through by a minority for the reason that there was no majority capable of doing it. If I had been born a Russian, I believe I could have adjusted myself to this condition.

It is not necessary, in establishing a world organization with a monopoly of military authority, to change the structure of the three great powers. It would be for the three individuals who draft the Constitution to devise ways for the different structures to be fitted together for collaboration.

Do I fear the tyranny of a World Government? Of course I do. But I fear still more the coming of another war or wars. Any government is certain to be evil to some extent. But a World Government is preferable to the far greater evil of wars, particularly with their intensified destructiveness. If a World Government is not established by agreement, I believe it will come in another way and in a much more dangerous form. For war or wars will end in one power's being supreme and dominating the rest of the world by its overwhelming military strength.

Time Is Essential

Now that we have the atomic secret, we must not lose it, and that is what we should risk doing if we should give it to the United Nations organization or to the Soviet Union. But we must make it clear, as quickly as possible, that we are not keeping the bomb a secret for the sake of our power, but in the hope of establishing peace in a World Government, and that we will do our utmost to bring this World Government into being.

I appreciate that there are persons who favor a gradual approach to World Government even though they approve of it as the ultimate objective. The trouble about taking little steps, one at a time, in the hope of reaching that ultimate goal is that while they are being taken, we continue to keep the bomb secret without making our reason convincing to those who do not have the secret. That of itself creates fear and suspicion, with the consequence that the relations of rival sovereignties deteriorate dangerously. So, while persons who take only a step at a time may think they are approaching world peace, they actually are contributing, by their slow pace, to the coming of war. We have no time to spend in this way. If war is to be averted, it must be done quickly.

Alliance for Peace

Since reason condemns war and makes peace an absolute duty, and since peace cannot be effected or guaranteed without a compact among nations, they must form an alliance of a peculiar kind, which may be called a pacific alliance, different from a treaty of peace, inasmuch as it would forever terminate all wars, whereas the latter only ends one.

Immanuel Kant, *Perpetual Peace*, 1795.

We shall not have the secret very long. I know it is argued that no other country has money enough to spend on the development of the atomic bomb, and this fact assures us the secret for a long time. It is a mistake often made in this country to measure things by the amount of money they cost. But other countries which have the materials and the men can apply them to the work of developing atomic power if they care to do so. For men and materials and the decision to use them, and not money, are all that is needed....

I myself do not have the gift of explanation by which to persuade large numbers of people of the urgencies of the problems the human race now faces. Hence I should like to command someone who has this gift of explanation—Emery Reves, whose book, *The Anatomy of Peace*, is intelligent, brief, clear, and, if I may use the abused term, dynamic on the topic of war and the need for World Government.

Since I do not foresee that atomic energy is to be a great boon for a long time, I have to say that for the present it is a menace. Perhaps it is well that it should be. It may intimidate the human race into bringing order into its international affairs, which, without the pressure of fear, it would not do.

"Any intervention...upon the part of...world government, in the internal affairs of independent peoples...would subject the nations of the world to a dictatorship exercised by the Big Three."

World Government Could Bring Slavery

Sumner Welles

Until his death in 1961, Sumner Welles was a distinguished public servant and a prolific author. He was ambassador to Cuba, assistant secretary of state and undersecretary of state during the administration of Franklin D. Roosevelt. Mr. Welles resigned from government in 1943 and devoted himself to lecturing and writing. His countless works include *World of the Four Freedoms* and *The Time for Decision*. In the following viewpoint, Mr. Welles claims that world government can be achieved only by subjugating the weaker nations of the world to the dictates of the powerful ones.

As you read, consider the following questions:

1. Why does Mr. Welles believe Russia would not participate in a world government?
2. Why does he believe Great Britain and the US would be unwilling to join?
3. Why does the author claim that Einstein's proposed world government would lead to international serfdom?

Sumner Welles, "The Atomic Bomb and World Government," *The Atlantic Monthly*, January 1946. Copyright © 1946 R 1974, by The Atlantic Monthly Company, Boston, MA. Reprinted by permission.

In the November [1945] issue of *Atlantic Monthly*, Professor Albert Einstein has given us his drastic and urgent recommendations as to the course we should follow in dealing with the problem of the atomic bomb.

Professor Einstein has played a notable part in the development of atomic energy. He figured prominently in the series of events which led to the manufacture of the atomic bomb. He is a citizen of the United States, and his fellow Americans are justly proud of his achievements. I regret the obligation under which I find myself of taking issue with many of the views and recommendations set forth in his article. Yet I must do so because I believe that many people who recognize the authority with which he speaks in the field of science will be readily persuaded that he is for that reason an equally competent guide in the field of international politics....

Professor Einstein...asserts: "It is not necessary, in establishing a world organization with a monopoly of military authority, to change the structure of the three great powers. It would be for the three individuals who draft the constitution to devise ways for the different structures to be fitted together for collaboration."

In Professor Einstein's view the solution is as simple as that. He is evidently confident that adoption of his proposal is not only imperative but feasible as well.

The question before us is whether his proposal is practicable and desirable.

I am convinced that the achievement of any such objective at this time is wholly impracticable. I must add that I also have grave questions as to the desirability of his proposal in the form in which he presents it.

Russia Would Not Participate

Professor Einstein's concept is premised upon his assumption that the Soviet Government would agree to a world government with power "over all military matters" provided the Soviet Government may prepare the first draft of a constitution for such a world government.

It is interesting to speculate as to the nature of the draft constitution which the Soviet Government would now prepare.

I can conceive of the Soviet Union's agreeing to enter a world government if a constitution is drafted, and is agreed upon by the United States and Great Britain, which provides for a World Union of Soviet Socialist Republics with the capital of that world government located in Moscow. I cannot imagine that the Soviet Union would participate in a world government upon any other basis.

No world government of the character envisaged by Professor Einstein could function unless it possessed the power to exercise complete control over the armaments of each constituent state, and unless every nation was willing to open up every inch of its territory and every one of its laboratories and factories to a continuing in-

Albert Einstein in 1953.

ternational inspection. Nor could it function unless the government of each participating country was equally willing to submit to the scrutiny of the authorities of the world government every one of its governmental processes, including its conduct of foreign and internal affairs and of finance.

It surely requires no demonstration that any such requisite as that would wholly destroy the present Soviet system. We have every right to believe, from our knowledge of Russian policy and from our understanding of the fundamental motives inherent in the Soviet form of Communism, that neither the present Soviet Government nor the rank and file of the members of the Communist party in Russia would ever consent to the obliteration, from one day to another, of the system which, over a period of twenty-eight years, they have at so great a sacrifice finally, with a great measure of success, established. We have every reason to be confident that unless the Soviet Union could so dominate the proposed world government as to preclude the possibility of any weakening of its own control of Russian foreign and domestic policy, it would not participate in that government.

Differences Are Too Great

And what about the United States and Great Britain?

We may, for the sake of argument, grant the highly unlikely possibility that a majority of the people of the United States would be willing to consider participation in a United States of the World built upon a foundation similar to that provided in their own Federal Constitution. It is within the realm of possibility that the British people would be willing to throw overboard their own form of government, although it has served them well and proved responsive to their own peculiar requirements, and join in such a United States of the World. But it is to my mind fantastic to assume that either the American or the British people would be willing to join in a World Union of Soviet Socialist Republics when such a union would inevitably result in the dissolution of the individual form of government which they have gradually evolved to meet their national needs, and also abolish all those cherished principles of individual liberty which are sacred to the Anglo-Saxon peoples— and which, in the case of the United States, are comprised in the Bill of Rights.

I believe that the major fallacy in Professor Einstein's proposal lies in his assertion that "it is not necessary, in establishing a world organization with a monopoly of military authority, to change the structure of the three great powers." I regard it as wholly impossible that the three individuals who, he suggests, should draft the constitution for this world government could, for the purposes he envisages, ever succeed in devising "ways for the different structures to be fitted together for collaboration."

Too High a Cost

There is another aspect of Professor Einstein's proposal which fills me with amazement. He declares that, in addition to the other powers with which he would vest his world government, that government should have "the power to intervene in countries where a minority is oppressing a majority and creating the kind of instability that leads to war." He admits that it is true that in the

Soviet Union the minority rules, but he insists that, if he had been born a Russian, he could have "adjusted" himself to this condition.

If I understand his thesis correctly, and I think I do, minority rule should be regarded as iniquitous in every nation of the world except the Soviet Union. His proposed world government would, therefore, be granted the right to intervene in every country of the earth for the purpose of establishing there such form of government, or such internal regime, as the dominating powers within the world government considered desirable, with the exception of the Soviet Union.

This view, of course approximates the classic thesis of the Third International that minorities are entitled to exercise control when they are of the Communist faith. Examples are not wanting that the logical outgrowth of this philosophy is the assertion of the right of Communist minorities by liquidations and terror to dominate opposing majorities until those majorities have been forced into the Communist line.

The issue raises one of the gravest problems with which freedom-loving people are today faced. Will peoples such as the English-speaking peoples, determined upon the preservation at any cost of their individual liberty, accept any form of world order which grants to some alien and superior power the authority to intervene in their internal life in such a manner as to determine for them how they shall be governed, to what extent their individual liberty may be reduced, and whether the voice of dissenting minorities or of dissenting majorities may make itself heard?

International Serfdom

I wholly agree that no peaceful world can be envisaged unless the nations which take part in a new international organization voluntarily fix certain standards of governmental conduct which they commit themselves severally to uphold. These standards must comprehend the assurance that religious and political freedom, and the chance to obtain economic security, will be guaranteed without discrimination to all their respective nationals. This international organization must see to it that the guaranties so fixed are carried out.

But any intervention, such as that which Professor Einstein proposes, upon the part of his world government, in the internal affairs of independent peoples, for the sole purpose of imposing upon them a standardized form of government or a particular brand of political philosophy, would subject the nations of the world to a dictatorship exercised by the Big Three, with all other peoples as abject serfs. No free world can be founded upon a such a concept. It was precisely in order to prevent the establishment of such a world that the vast majority of the United Nations fought through to final victory over the Axis powers.

146

"We can perform a great service to ourselves and to the cause of world peace by refuting the notion that the highest value is absolute national sovereignty."

World Federalism Is Possible

Norman Cousins

Editor of the *Saturday Review* since 1942, Norman Cousins is a world recognized spokesperson for internationalism. He was a member of the Commission to Study Organized Peace, founder and president of the United World Federalists and cochairman of the National Committee for a Sane Nuclear Policy. Cousins has labored tirelessly for the cause of world peace through world government and has authored numerous books on the subject including *Modern Man Is Obsolete* (1945), *In Place of Folly* (1961), and *The Human Option* (1981). In the following viewpoint, Mr. Cousins draws a parallel between the successful federation of America's original thirteen colonies and the possible federation of the world community of nations.

As you read, consider the following questions:

1. What does the author claim was the American Founding Fathers' main contribution to history?
2. How does the author compare the American situation between 1783 and 1789 to the current world situation?

Norman Cousins, "Reflections on a Birthday," *Saturday Review*. Reprinted with permission from *Saturday Review* and Norman Cousins.

The range of America's contribution to history...runs broad and deep, but the idea that ultimately may have the single greatest impact on the world is that human beings are capable of designing a rational future. The specific expression of that capability in this nation was the United States Constitution. This country was not the first in history to devise a representative government, but no other society was more carefully constructed for the express purpose of making representative government work.

The fact that the United States has lived longer under a single continuous form of government than has any other major nation is a tribute to that design. The U.S. Constitution was a piece of political architecture specifically intended to withstand the stresses and flaws that throughout history had caused other governments to become erratic or irresponsible or to turn against their own people. The American idea that government could be constructed as an act of intelligence and free will has inspired countless peoples and has produced more change in the world than any other political or even ideological concept, not excluding Marxism.

Difficulties in Early America

The design of the young American Founding Fathers was not struck off overnight. It took two years to hammer out that design and to put it into effect. Each problem and challenge had to be examined in the light of historical experience and common sense. Failures of previous governments became the raw materials for constructing a durable new model. Of all these failures, none was more dramatic, significant, or insistent than the collapse of the American states themselves in their ill-fated experience before federation.

This failure, indeed, was to serve as the impetus for the enduring structure that became the United States; but the fact and implications of that failure are not generally understood today by Americans themselves.

The popular notion about the origin of the United States government is that the Declaration of Independence and the United States Constitution were part of a single historical process. This misconception is reflected in the Bicentennial celebration itself. The United States will not be 200 years old in 1976. The United States was not born until 1789. The nation will not have its Bicentennial until 1989. This is not a historical quibble. There were years of deterioration and disintegration after the end of the Revolution before the U.S. Constitution came into being.

Before the United States could be born, the 13 sovereign American governments had to undergo a collapse of mammoth proportions. John Fiske, in *The Critical Period of American History, 1783-1789*, has written a sobering account of this collapse. The 13 states thought they could retain predominant sovereignty and still be at peace with one another. After 1783, when the treaty was signed with England, the American states slid into a period of disruption bordering on anarchy. New York and New Jersey shot it out in the harbor over the right to tax incoming ships. Pennsylvania and New Jersey never could agree on a mutually satisfactory border. Connecticut and Massachusetts were at odds over the acquisition of western territories. The value of a citizen's currency would shrink 10 percent when he or she crossed a state line. Thus a citizen who started out from New Hampshire with $100 in his pocket would have $20.24 left by the time he arrived in Georgia—without having spent a cent.

A Federal System of Government

Men of reason were convinced that it was a fallacy to suppose that 13 separate sovereign states could exist within a compressed geographic unit. They came together at Philadelphia in 1787 because the situation confronting the states was intolerable. They had no way of knowing whether they could create a new design acceptable to each of the separate states. But they hoped that the results of their efforts might produce a groundswell of popular support that would create an imperative for ratification by the individual legislatures.

Unity in Freedom

In urging progress toward a world community, I cite the American concept of the destiny of a progressive society. Here in this land, in what was once a wilderness, we have generated a society and a civilization drawn from many sources. Yet out of the mixture of many peoples and faiths we have developed unity in freedom—a unity designed to protect the rights of each individual while enhancing the freedom and well-being of all.

This concept of unity in freedom, drawn from the diversity of many racial strains and cultures, we would like to see made a reality for all mankind....

Thus we see as our goal, not a superstate above nations but a world community embracing them all, rooted in law and justice and enhancing the potentialities and common purposes of all peoples.

Dwight D. Eisenhower, in a speech to the General Assembly of the UN, September 22, 1960.

The most distinctive feature of the document created at Philadelphia was its federalist principles. The individual states retained jursidiction over their own territories while yielding authority on all matters concerned with common dangers and common needs. This meant that a central authority spoke and acted for all the states in their collective relationship to the rest of the world.

The main contribution to history of the American Founding

Fathers, therefore, was their delineation of the principles by which peace among sovereign units could be created and maintained. They had studied the basic causes of war all the way back to the conflict between Athens and Sparta. They understood the imperatives of geography. They knew that the freedoms of the individual would erode without a structured framework of order for society itself.

World-Wide Federalism

The fact that our national Bicentennial birthday is not in 1976 but in 1989 is not so important as our ability to understand the principles that went into the making of this nation. Those principles are no less valid now than they were 200 years ago. The peace of the world today is precarious because many of the sovereign units, especially the major ones, are unwilling to accept, or even to consider, the principles that alone can establish workable world order and thus guarantee their peace and independence. The United States, against the background of its history and traditions, has a natural reason to proclaim these principles. We can perform a great service to ourselves and to the cause of world peace by refuting the notion that the highest value is absolute national sovereignty. We can carry the banner for the idea that world peace cannot be achieved, nor the natural rights of human beings protected and enlarged, without a genuine world order.

It will be said that to draw a parallel between the failures of the American states from 1783 to 1787 and the United Nations' situation today is to overstretch historical analogy. It will be claimed that the hundreds or so sovereignties in the present world are too diffuse, too farflung, too complex, to be compared with the 13 states. But one can almost hear James Madison or Alexander Hamilton saying, as they did in *The Federalist Papers*, that historical principles transcend the size and complexity of the case at hand. The larger the problem, they said, the more pertinent the principle. And the principle that informed their efforts at Philadelphia, and that has meaning for us today, is that the only way to eliminate anarchy is by establishing law. They would say that the only security for Americans today, or for any people, is in the creation of a system of world order that enables nations to retain sovereignty over their cultures and institutions but that creates a workable authority for regulating the behavior of the nations in their relationships with one another. They would recognize the mountainous complexities to be surmounted, but they would also believe that there are nuclear imperatives which dictate the need for world law.

World federalism may seem too remote a goal to serve as the basis for immediate efforts. But a world that is ingenious enough to create the means of nuclear incineration ought to be resourceful enough to devise a way out with a time schedule to match.

6
VIEWPOINT

"We find that true peace quite easily exists
between nations which are not federated."

World Federalism
Will Not Work

G. Edward Griffin

A conservative writer and graduate of the University of Michigan,
G. Edward Griffin has lectured throughout the US in opposition
to the United Nations and America's membership in the world
body. He has worked in television, film production, and public
relations, and has authored *The Life and Words of Robert Welch,
Founder of the John Birch Society* and *The Fearful Master: A Second
Look at the United Nations*. In the following viewpoint, Mr. Griffin argues that analogies favorably comparing the federation of
the original thirteen colonies with the United Nations' potential
for achieving a workable world federalism are invalid and
dangerous.

As you read, consider the following questions:

1. Why does the author claim that America's success with
   federalism does not guarantee the success of world
   federalism?
2. How does the author think world peace can be realized?

G. Edward Griffin, *The Fearful Master: A Second Look at the United Nations*, Belmont: Western
Islands Publishing Co., 1964. Reprinted by permission of the publisher, Western Islands,
Belmont, MA 02178.

The UN is merely doing between nations what we did so successfully with our thirteen colonies. This, in essence, is the plea for federalism, and is based on the idea that the mere act of joining separate political units together into a larger federal entity will somehow prevent those units from waging war with each other. The success of our own federal system is most often cited as proof that this theory is valid. But such an evaluation is a shallow one. First of all, the American Civil War, one of the most bloody in all history, illustrates conclusively that the mere federation of governments, even those culturally similar, as in America, does not automatically prevent war between them. Secondly, we find that true peace quite easily exists between nations which are *not* federated. As a matter of fact, members of the British Commonwealth of Nations seemed to get along far more peacefully after the political bonds between them had been relaxed. In other words, true peace has absolutely nothing to do with whether separate political units are joined together—except, perhaps, that such a union may create a common military defense sufficiently impressive to deter an aggressive attack. But that is peace between the union and outside powers; it has little effect on peace between the units, themselves, which is the substance of the UN argument.

Federalism: Tyranny of the Majority

Peace is the natural result of relationships between groups and cultures which are mutually satisfactory to both sides. These relationships are found with equal ease within or across federal lines. As a matter of fact, they are the same relationships that promote peaceful conditions within the community, the neighborhood, the family itself. What are they? Just stop and think for a moment; if you were marooned on an island with two other people, what relationships between you would be mutually satisfactory enough to prevent you from resorting to violence in your relationships? Or, to put it the other way around, what would cause you to break the peace and raise your hand against your partners?

Obviously, if one or both of the others attempted to seize your food and shelter, you would fight. Their reaction to similar efforts on your part would be the same. If they attempted to take away your freedom, to dictate how you should conduct your affairs, or tell you what moral and ethical standards you must follow, likewise, you would fight. And if they constantly ridiculed your attire, your manners and your speech, in time you might be sparked into a brawl. The best way to keep the peace on that island is for each one to mind his own business, to respect each other's right to his own property, to respect the other fellow's right to be different (even to act in a way that seems foolish or improper, if he wishes), to have compassion for each other's troubles and hardships—but to *force* each other to do nothing! And, to make sure that the others hold to their end of the bargain, each should keep physically strong enough to make any violation of this code unprofitable.

Now, suppose these three got together and decided to form a political union, to "federate," as it were. Would this really change anything? Suppose they declared themselves to be the United Persons, and wrote a charter, and held daily meetings, and passed resolutions. What then? These superficial ceremonies might be fun for a while, but the minute two of them out-voted the other and started "legally" to take his food and shelter, limit his freedom, or force him to accept an unwanted standard of moral conduct, they would be right back where they all began. Charter or no charter they would fight.

Increasing the Danger of War

In the United Nations, there are precious few common bonds that could help overcome the clash of cross-purposes that inevitably must arise between groups with such divergent ethnic, linguistic, legal, religious, cultural and political environments. To add fuel to the fire, the UN concept is one of unlimited governmental power to impose by force a monolithic set of values and conduct on all groups and individuals whether they like it or not. Far from insuring peace, such conditions can only enhance the chances of war.

G. Edward Griffin.

Is it really different between nations? Not at all. The same simple code of conduct applies in all human relationships, large or small. Regardless of the size, be it international or three men on an island, the basic unit is still the human personality. Ignore this fact, and any plan is doomed to failure.

Colonial America and the UN

When the thirteen colonies formed our Federal Union, they had two very important factors in their favor, neither of which are present in the United Nations. First, the colonies themselves were all of a similar cultural background. They enjoyed similar legal systems, they spoke the same language, and they shared similar religious beliefs. They had much in common. The second advantage, and the most important of the two, was that they formed their union under a constitution which was designed to prevent any of them, *or a majority of them*, from forcefully intervening in the affairs of the others. The original federal government was authorized to provide mutual defense, run a post office, and that was about all. As previously mentioned, however, even though we had these powerful forces working in our favor, full scale war did break out at one tragic point in our history.

The peace that followed, of course, was no peace at all, but was only the smoldering resentment and hatred that falls in the wake of any armed conflict. Fortunately, the common ties between North and South, the cultural similarities and the common heritage, have proved through the intervening years to overbalance the differences. And with the gradual passing away of the generation that carried the battle scars, the Union has healed.

In the United Nations, there are precious few common bonds that could help overcome the clash of cross-purposes that inevitably must arise between groups with such divergent ethnic, linguistic, legal, religious, cultural and political environments. To add fuel to the fire, the UN concept is one of unlimited governmental power to impose by force a monolithic set of values and conduct on all groups and individuals whether they like it or not. Far from insuring peace, such conditions can only enhance the chances of war.

7

"The strongest argument for global integration is a negative one: without it, humanity is doomed to suffer even more wars that will become increasingly lethal, culminating in holocaust."

The Promise of World Government

Sidney Lens

Sidney Lens is an outspoken labor leader and activist in peace and radical movements. He is a lecturer on foreign policy and contributing editor to *The Progressive, Liberation,* and numerous other magazines and newspapers. Mr. Lens authored several books including *Unrepentant Radical, The Bomb* and *The Maginot Line Syndrome: America's Hopeless Foreign Policy.* In the following viewpoint, Mr. Lens outlines what he believes is a credible, although difficult, program for establishing world government.

As you read, consider the following questions:

1. Why does the author cite statistics by Quincy Wright and the Stockholm International Peace Institute?
2. What does the author mean by "disarmament"?
3. What role does the author believe multinational corporations should play in a new system of world government?

Sidney Lens, "World Government Reconsidered," *The Nation*, September 17, 1983. Reprinted with permission, *The Nation* magazine, Nation Associates, Inc. © 1983.

155

World government is an idea whose time has come. It is not yet on everyone's lips, any more than the idea of a United States of America was on the lips of our forebears in 1750. But its coming is dictated by history. It is the logical next step in the social evolution of the human species beyond the nation-state. In the past it was simply considered desirable by certain philosophers. It was embodied in socialist and communist manifestoes (though upon achieving power, adherents of neither sought to implement the idea, or even discuss it) and preached by the United World Federalists. Now, however, it has become indispensable to the survival of civilization.

The strongest argument for global integration is a negative one: without it, humanity is doomed to suffer even more wars that will become increasingly lethal, culminating in holocaust in the not-too-distant future. In the age of the nation-state, war has been the final arbiter of international disputes. According to historian Quincy Wright, there were 278 wars between 1480 and 1941; other authorities put the count higher. The Stockholm International Peace Institute estimates that since 1945, there have been 140 "little" wars, which took a toll of 30 million to 50 million lives....

What Opponents Say

[Therefore] the question is not whether world government is necessary, but how to achieve it and how to make it work. All sorts of objections can be raised to the idea....It is said that world government is not realistic under present circumstances. The United States might be willing to swallow Canada and Mexico as the fifty-first and fifty-second states, but its citizens would not accept an international government dominated by communist, socialist and Third World countries. Another objection is that nationalism has not played out its string—a sizable majority of the world's people have experienced their national revolutions only in the past forty years and would probably be unwilling to give up even a measure of their hard-won independence. Another objection is that world government would weaken social cohesion. "Social cohesion, insofar as it is instinctive," Bertrand Russell says in his book *Has Man a Future?*, "is mainly promoted by a common danger or a common enemy." With no "out-groups" to hate, the social bonds would loosen. Still another objection is that world government is unattainable because human beings are reluctant to plunge into the unknown; the nation-state may be an impediment to progress, but we are accustomed to it. "Better the devil you know...." Perhaps the greatest problem is that of uniting the divergent social systems that have grown up under communism and capitalism (e.g., Chinese, Yugoslav, Russian and Hungarian communism; American, German, Japanese and Swedish capitalism).

There is some merit to each of these objections, yet as a whole they are overdrawn. Certainly there is a danger of despotism, but the world military force would be considerably smaller than the combined armies of the present nation-states, because it would come into being after their military forces had been disbanded and because its only task would be to intervene in situations where police forces could not keep order. It would not need nuclear weapons or other sophisticated machines of war to perform that limited function. As the feasibility of making a quantum jump from nation-states to a single world-state, humankind has made similar

THERE OUGHT TO BE A LAW!

Justus in the *Minneapolis Star.* Reprinted by permission.

jumps before—in response to the discovery of fire, the development of agriculture and the advent of the Industrial Revolution. Those changes were severe—but humanity survived, and in fact thrived. In May 1945, Secretary of War Henry L. Stimson called the atomic bomb "a revolutionary change in the relations between man and the universe," and his description still holds. Ending the threat of nuclear holocaust calls for social changes greater than any humanity has ever known.

Apply Human Intelligence

A world without war and bitter hatred seems almost inconceivable, yet as individuals we sublimate our aggressions every day. Most of us live out our entire life without killing a single person. We express hatred verbally, not physically. An animal as intelligent as the human animal should, with time, effort and education, be able to suppress the "will to hurt."

The problem of blending the world's various social forms is more formidable—but not insuperable, providing the process takes place over a long period of time. In fact, both communism and capitalism are already on the threshold of profound changes. Communism cannot survive unless it decentralizes its economy (as Yugoslavia has done, and Hungary, to a degree, and as China is now attempting to do) and encourages greater popular participation in state planning; and capitalism cannot survive unless it moves toward a planned economy and distributes the fruits of labor more equitably. In the course of disarmament and the creation of supranational bodies, the differences between the two systems will be reduced as each recognizes that neither communism nor capitalism can survive a nuclear war, and adjusts accordingly.

The most sensible approach to world government is to combine ironclad commitments from the powers capable of making it a reality with a slow pace toward that goal. While it might have been possible in 1945 for the United States, Britain and the Soviet Union—the only nations with significant military forces—to impose world government in one fell swoop, it is not possible today. There are many additional hurdles to jump—many more nationalisms to deal with and economic problems to solve. Achieving world government must be a measured process, beginning with disarmament.

A Broader Disarmament

Disarmament, it should be noted, is not just a matter of destroying bombs and demobilizing troops. It has an inner logic of its own, each step leading to the next. In the process of rearmament after World War II, the United States constructed a "national security state" by establishing agencies such as the National Security Council, the Central Intelligence Agency and the National Security Agency. Disarmament requires the liquidation of those agencies and the creation of others to deal with different kinds of problems. If nations are to eliminate their bombs and troops, they must have alternate means of settling their disputes. The formation of an international police force, which was once contemplated by the United Nations, would be imperative. The World Court as currently constituted but with real powers, or a new one, would adjudicate international disputes, and its decisions would be backed by the international police force.

Why War?

Why do wars occur? Because of a combination of two things: (1) conflicts of interest between people in one country and people in another, leading to disputes, and (2) the lack of any effective peaceful machinery for settling disputes—machinery that nations can be compelled to use.

Conflicts of interest, and therefore disputes, are inevitable. But the lack of a required method of settling disputes peacefully has given nations no alternative to that of acquiring military power and then using diplomacy backed by stated or implied threats of force to gain a favorable settlement, and if that isn't successful, waging war.

Lawrence Abbott, *World Federalism: What? Why? How?* 1977.

The disarmament phase would be an ideal time to set up supranational bodies with the power to perform certain functions worldwide, in line with the proposals made by U.N. Secretary General U Thant in 1969. U Thant suggested the formation of four international bodies to monitor pollution, population, poverty and the proliferation of nuclear weapons. Each would be given sovereign powers to enforce its decisions in every country, and presumably would be backed by the international police force. They might stop plutonium production, for instance, or impose limits on population growth. U Thant's idea is not as farfetched as it sounds. Indeed, the United States proposed a similar plan thirty-seven years ago, at a U.N. disarmament conference. Bernard Baruch, the U.S. representative, suggested the formation of an International Atomic Development Authority, which would assume "various forms of ownership, dominion, licenses, operation, inspection, research, and management" of everything associated with atomic energy, including nuclear weapons....

As the world begins to disarm, the Soviet Union would lose its hold over Eastern Europe, and the United States would lose its hold over its client states. Each superpower would have to adjust its economy accordingly. Without far-flung military bases, a Navy second to none and the C.I.A., the United States would not be able to guarantee the security of private foreign investment or the access

159

to raw materials and trade that U.S. multinational corporations now enjoy. That would create the twin problems of determining what to do with those corporations and how to restructure U.S. relations with the Third World.

The multinationals are the foundation of Western militarism and the established order. There can be no significant change so long as they retain their present power. The major corporations and industries—oil, banking, the utilities, etc.—would have to be placed under social ownership, and smaller firms under social control. Admittedly that is a revolutionary step, but the nuclear age is the most revolutionary one in history; it requires comparable social changes. Whether the owners of large corporations should be compensated, and if so, how much, are pragmatic questions to be answered as circumstances require.

Of greater concern is deciding how to use the facilities of the dismantled multinationals to benefit the people of the Third World. The U.S. government could use those facilities in partnership with Third World countries. In one of the many possible scenarios, the United States would provide the operating capital and the supervisory personnel for these "fifty-fifty" companies in return for a small percentage of any profits. The home government would be given 50 percent of the stock, and its citizens would be trained to take over the managerial posts. After ten or fifteen years, the facilities and all the stock would be turned over to the Third World government. This type of aid has not been tried extensively, but there are a few examples to draw on: Israel helped Ghana develop its shipping industry under such an arrangement, and Britain and Burma cooperated in a similar fashion to build the latter's mining industry.

A Slow Process

The implementation of world government would not only require the formation of planning agencies to help the industrial powers make the transition; it would impose an obligation on the advanced nations to help the Third World become economically viable. The United States—ideally with Soviet support—could help the less developed nations establish "customs unions." By eliminating trade barriers, the customs unions would assure larger markets for the products of small countries. They would also promote greater efficiency and higher standards of living in the less developed countries. Inevitably, there would be economic dislocations. Less efficient companies would go out of business, while more efficient ones would prosper. Some international body would have to subsidize displaced workers and companies. After a customs union had been in operation for some time, its members might be combined in a single *inter*-nation, a United States of Central America, a United States of North Africa, a United States of Southeast Asia. It is impossible to predict how long that process would take, but the formation of such inter-nations would be a major way station on the road to world government.

It would be misleading to minimize the problems connected with world government. It is terra incognita, just as capitalism was in the latter days of feudalism. The various proposals for supranational government put forth since 1945 are necessarily too schematic, too simplistic, too general. They do not supply the answers to scores of problems.

But that does not mean the goal of world government is unrealistic. It means that the world should move toward it slowly, grappling with now unforeseeable problems as they arise. The goal itself can no longer be questioned. Though most of us do not yet want to accept it, the nation-state and the war system it has spawned are obsolete. Whatever the trials and tribulations involved in fashioning a world-state, humanity has no other recourse if it wishes to survive. It is a matter of "one world or none."

8

> *"Surely world government is an idea...whose time came forty years ago and has long since gone."*

The Flaws in World Government

Richard Falk and Kirkpatrick Sale

The following viewpoint offers two replies to Sidney Lens' arguments advocating world government. The first was authored by Richard Falk, a member of the editorial board of *The Nation* magazine. Mr. Falk is also Albert G. Milbank Professor of international law and practice at Princeton University. The second is by Kirkpatrick Sale, the author of *Power Shift* and *Human Scale*. Mr. Sale is currently at work on a book about American regionalism. Both authors are critical of the promise of world government and essentially argue that world government could possibly initiate a broader range of problems than it proposes to eliminate.

As you read, consider the following questions:

1. What does Mr. Falk mean when he writes that part of his concern with world government is "merely semantic"?
2. Why does Mr. Sale believe that the idea of an end to war is a foolish notion?
3. What are some of the historical examples Mr. Sale offers to support his arguments?
4. Do you agree with Mr. Lens or the authors of this viewpoint? Why?

Richard Falk and Kirkpatrick Sale, "Replies," *The Nation*, September 17, 1983. Reprinted with permission, *The Nation* magazine, Nation Associates, Inc. © 1983.

I

Upon first reading Sidney Lens's essay, I was astonished to find that he had unabashedly joined the ranks of true believers in world government. After all, Lens is no starry-eyed, woolly-minded do-gooder who believes that something reasonable can be made to happen on the basis of a good argument. In both his life and his writings he has shown an acute awareness that reformist politics necessarily involve conflict and struggle. Therefore, his ideas cannot be dismissed as Enlightenment foolishness, of which the United World Federalists are the leading example.

Lens knows what the realization of world government would entail, including a program of social justice that would mobilize the resources of the rich for the benefit of humanity as a whole. His insistence on taking that path arises directly from his negative certainty: if the superpowers continue to put their faith in nuclear deterrence, a global catastrophe is bound to occur. There is only one way to avoid such a catastrophe, he says: political unification, which would require the creation of global institutions to settle disputes peacefully. Lens is aware of the obstacles his ideas will face, and he realizes that the leaders of sovereign nations will pay little heed to appeals to show concern for human survival.

The Bishops Speak

The Catholic bishops' pastoral letter on nuclear weapons talks of a "new moment" and of the task of creating a positive peace. Underlying the antinuclear movement is an awareness of human solidarity, of a common destiny that is more significant than differences of nationality, ideology, culture, religion or race. Is "world government" the best rallying cry to mobilize those who are alarmed and appalled by the indecencies, the dangers and the side effects (including the erosion of political democracy) of a continuing nuclear arms race? Possibly. After all, such a rallying cry does offer a vision, or at least a conception, of a new way of organizing world society. The idea of world government also challenges the illusion that catastrophe can be staved off by small steps (nuclear freeze, no first use). By its very nature, it implies forms of security different from those that exist in the present system, in which rival states rely on war machines and military alliances.

Despite these arguments, I remain skeptical. Part of my concern is merely semantic. The advocacy of world government has come to be associated primarily with the United States. Elsewhere, it is regarded either as a sterile notion or as part of America's imperial design. Because of those connotations, the term "world government" is not the proper linguistic package for the message of political unification. I have no satisfactory substitute, but some possibilities are "humane governance" or "just world polity," which do not arouse those negative associations.

But my doubts about world government go beyond semantics, to substance. Its proponents say that the solution to the problems of a world order premised on "parts" (states or regions or empires) is a large-scale, centralized bureaucracy. But as bureaucratic structures become more centralized they also become more oppressive. The fundamental precondition for a politics of survival is the emergence of a sense of global identity, accompanied by a new set of values, including nonviolence, resource sharing, conservation of the environment and respect for the dignity of all peoples. Once this revolution in consciousness has coalesced into a social movement, leaders will certainly appear. The old order will resist and the struggle will be joined. Those who are committed to reshaping the world's political structures will propose new international arrangements to sustain the necessary degree of political unification. But the nature of those arrangements must emerge from the process of struggle and must be determined by the participants and their leaders. "Government" should be regarded less as the goal, the mechanism, the solution, than as the minimal institutional expression of a new global political culture.

Back to Square One

If we ask what the nearest thing to a realizable world government today would be, the answer obviously is a joint U.S.-Soviet world empire (perhaps on the model of the Austro-Hungarian empire before World War I). That would involve dividing the world into two spheres, each run by one superpower acting in concert with the other. Under this arrangement the global police force...would consist of two contingents armed in accordance with agreements concluded by the two superpowers, which would be charged with maintaining law and order in their respective spheres.

Since we already know pretty much what the U.S. and Soviet conceptions of law and order amount to, it is easy to see that world government in present-day conditions would mean putting the world into two straitjackets. Sooner or later the result would be explosions, rebellions, civil wars and quite likely the breakup of the system itself. In other words, we would be back to square one, facing essentially the same problems we face today.

Doesn't it make more sense to try to understand and deal with these problems now rather than later?

Paul M. Sweezy, *The Nation*, September 17, 1983.

Perhaps nothing I have said is alien to what Sidney Lens believes. We have similar worries about the world situation, and we do not differ, really, in our belief that a way out exists. Where we do differ is on the matter of whether "world government" is the best name for what we want.

II

Surely world government is an idea—or, perhaps better, a posture—whose time came forty years ago and has long since gone. One would have thought that the global predicament to which the enormous and enormously powerful twentieth-century superstates have brought us—a world of insecurity, war, pollution, unremitting poverty and malnutrition, economic instability and political chaos—would be incontrovertible proof that increasing the size of governments is hardly the way to solve human problems. Indeed, as a moment's reflection suggests, it actually multiplies and exacerbates them. The present world organization, a trillion-dollar exercise in trivia and ineptitutde, gives no support to the idea that a single global institution can solve problems for 4.5 billion people.

Will Not End War

Though in the Lens view world government is supposed to cure every human ill, its principal function—its raison d'être—is apparently to end wars, and specifically to avert the nuclear one that now threatens us. But if Lens has really studied Quincy Wright, he must know that in the history of humankind larger and ever-larger governments have not *ended* wars, they have *created* them. War is the health of the state, it has been said, and the frequency, duration and severity of wars have increased in almost direct proportion to the increase in state size and power. (See, for example, Tables 22-54 in Wright's *A Study of War*.) A world state with an "international police force" empowered to enforce decisions by intervening in every country on every matter from birth control to death rates, which Lens and U Thant seem to have in mind, is a profoundly chilling prospect. That is not a way to end wars; it is a way to manipulate and escalate them so as to produce violence all over the globe.

Nor does the contemporary nation-state provide a good example of how to end violence. It is simply not true that "the state, with a monopoly of the means of violence, can enforce the peace between its citizens." If it could, we would not have the ugly murder and assault rates we have, the continuing organized crime wars, the urban gang battles, the K.K.K. assaults and all the rest of the individual and group violence that is common to America. And though Truman was right in saying that in America the states have not gone to war with one another for a long time, the same restraint cannot be found in many other nations—as the recent internecine warfare in Ethiopia, Ireland, Lebanon, Iran, Nicaragua, El Salvador, the Philippines and India demonstrates.

No, there is no earthly reason to think that a world government would "do away with war." Indeed, I think the idea of an end to war is a particularly foolish, perhaps dangerous, chimera. Aggression at some level may be, as most anthropologists agree, innate, and it is certainly true that humankind has always waged wars of one kind or another. But humanity has survived because for most of the 10,000 years we have been living in societies, we have worked to keep those wars as small and as harmless and as ritualized as possible.

Scale Down Conflicts

The logic is inescapable. It is not war that we should seek to eliminate but the awful, imbecilic, world-threatening *scale* of it. And the only way to do that is by reducing, not increasing, the scale of the participants. It is only by the division of nation-states into coherent regions, the political enactment of the separatist pulls and passions that exist everywhere in the world, that there is any chance of limiting state power and reducing the devastations of war. Division, not enlargement, is the solution: as in the human body, cells that divide are normal and healthy, those that agglomerate are cancerous.

Lest we forget: when Germany was divided into dozens of principalities and duchies and margravates, from about the twelfth century to the nineteenth, the Germans were the most pacific people in Europe. Germany participated in only thirteen wars while the aggrandizing nation-states of France, England and Spain each engaged in more than forty. When the people of Germany were united in an empire of tens of millions covering thousands of square miles, they became the instigators of a series of wars and colonial conquests, culminating in the two most destructive wars in history.

Lessons of History

Moreover, it can only be by the division of nation-states that we will begin to create conditions of social harmony rather than social conflict. As is the case with animals, humans tend to become more violent when they live under conditions of great stress, overcrowding and sensory overload; when stabilizing social and family processes are weakened; when rapid and heedless change creates fragile and unstable ecosystems; and when they become dependent on larger, more complex and more uncontrollable organizations within and among nations. Throughout history, societies that on a modest scale have achieved social coherence, political participation, cultural harmony and material balance have avoided war. Small states do not usually amass the kinds of riches that entice invaders. They choose not to divert scarce economic resources to expensive weaponry. And they realize far more acutely than do large nations the unbearable price of war and its preparations.

One last point. If, as Lens says, world government can come about only *after* world disarmament, the dissolution of the Soviet and American empires, the advent of democracy in Communist states and equality of distribution in capitalist ones, and the elimination of rapacious multinational corporations, *why bother*

166

with it? Even its most ardent advocates must appreciate that, at *that* time, it simply would no longer be necessary. Saying that the way to achieve world government is to accomplish a string of beautiful but unlikely reforms is begging the question. It is akin to saying that the way to get to heaven is to be born there.

Neither logic nor experience points us in the direction of larger governments, more complex systems, more elaborate methods of control, more powerful "peace forces." To continue to push this cause, in the face of the clear lessons of history and the clear evidence of the contemporary world, strikes me as being not only futile but possibly dangerous. For, if successful, I'm afraid we would get not only Einstein's tyranny of world government but, part and parcel, the very wars we want to avoid.

Distinguishing Between Fact and Opinion

This activity is designed to help develop the basic reading and thinking skill of distinguishing between fact and opinion. Consider the following statement as an example: "The United Nations Charter was signed on June 26, 1945." This statement is a fact easily verified in many history books. But consider another statement about the United Nations: "The UN will never be the insurance against war it was meant to be." This statement, because it lies in the realm of speculation cannot be verified. It is someone's opinion.

When investigating controversial issues it is important that one be able to distinguish between statements of fact and statements of opinion. It is also important to recognize that not all statements of fact are true. They may appear to be true, but some are based on inaccurate or false information. For this activity, however, we are concerned with understanding the difference between those statements which appear to be factual and those which appear to be based primarily on opinion.

Most of the following statements are taken from the viewpoints in this chapter. Consider each statement carefully. *Mark O for any statement you believe is an opinion or interpretation of facts. Mark F for any statement you believe is a fact.*

If you are doing this activity as a member of a class or group, compare your answers with those of other class or group members. Be able to defend your answers. You may discover that others will come to different conclusions than you. Listening to the reasons others present for their answers may give you valuable insights in distinguishing between fact and opinion.

If you are reading this book alone, ask others if they agree with your answers. You too will find this interaction very valuable.

O = *opinion*
F = *fact*

1. The only possible response true to our nature as social animals is the building of a world civilization.
2. Nuclear holocaust is such a threat that our survival as a race is intellectually improbable.
3. According to government calculations, the nuclear arms we possess at this time could destroy the earth.
4. Neither the Soviet Union nor the United States is likely to submit to a world government controlled by the other.
5. The United World Federalists is an organization devoted to the cause of world government.
6. The Soviet Union has used its veto power in the Security Council more often than the United States.
7. Albert Einstein played a notable part in the development of atomic energy.
8. We will never persuade the Soviets to join a non-communist world government.
9. Einstein advocated that a world government should be founded by the United States, the Soviet Union, and Great Britian.
10. The United Nations is composed of many different agencies.
11. As long as there are sovereign nations possessing great power, war is inevitable.
12. The Stockholm International Peace Institute estimates that since 1945, there have been 140 "little" wars.
13. An end to non-intervention will help keep peace.
14. World government is the logical next step in the social evolution of the human species.
15. An animal as intelligent as the human animal should be able to suppress the "will to hurt."
16. After World War II, the United States established the National Security Council and the National Security Agency.
17. The US has suggested the formation of an International Atomic Development Authority, but such an organization has never materialized.
18. Both communism and capitalism are on the threshold of profound changes.
19. The nuclear age is the most revolutionary one in history.

Bibliography

The following list of books, periodicals, and pamphlets deals with the subject matter of this chapter.

Lawrence Abbott	*World Federalism: What? Why? How?* Pamphlet available from World Federalist Association, 418 Seventh St. SE, Washington, DC 20003.
David Armstrong	*The Rise of International Organizations.* New York: St. Martin's Press, 1983.
Walter Berns	"The New Pacifism and World Government," *National Review*, May 27, 1983.
Hedley Bull	*The Anarchical Society: A Study of Order in World Politics.* New York: Columbia University Press, 1977.
Grenville Clark and Louis Sohn	*Introduction to World Peace Through World Law.* Chicago: World Without War Publications, revised 1984 edition.
Inis Claude Jr.	*Swords into Plowshares: The Problems and Progress of International Organizations.* New York: Random House, 1971.
Richard N. Cooper	*Toward a Renovated International System.* New York: Trilateral Commission, 1977.
Norman Cousins	*Modern Man Is Obsolete.* New York: Viking Press, 1945.
Albert Einstein and Sigmund Freud	*Why War?* Paris: International Institute of Intellectual Co-operation, 1933.
Richard A. Falk	*Toward a Just World Order.* Boulder, CO: Westview Press, 1982.
Herbert C. Hoover and H. Gibson	*Problems of Lasting Peace.* White Plains, NY: Kraus International Publications, 1969.
Thomas L. Hughes	"The Twilight of Internationalism," *Foreign Policy*, Winter 1985/1986.
Helmut Schmidt	*The Anachronism of National Strategy: The Reality of Interdependence.* New Haven, CT: Yale University Press, 1986.
Julius Stone	*Visions of World Order: Between State Power and Human Justice.* Baltimore: Johns Hopkins University Press, 1984.

Index

173

61, 63
as against free enterprise, 64-65
as exculsive, 65, 80
as necessary, 53-57, 67-72, 73-78
as promoting conflict, 58-61, 64-66, 79-86
as promoting harmony, 53-57, 67-72, 73-78, 81
as unnecessary, 62-66, 79-86
blocs of, 82-84
Campaign for UN Reform, 78
conferences of, 75
funding of, 81-82
General Assembly, 63, 64, 69, 77, 82, 113
origins of, 80-81
policymaking, 66
potential collapse of, 86
principles of, 68
purposes of, 56, 60, 68, 84
Security Council, 66, 69, 80, 82, 134
United Nations Educational, Scientific and Cultural Organization (UNESCO), 65, 72, 74
United States
and International Monetary Fund, 105-107, 110, 113, 115, 117, 120, 121
and League of Nations, 19-22, 23-27
and noninterference, 24
and the World Bank, 99
and world government, 134, 135, 138, 143, 145, 147-150, 163, 164
Constitution, 148, 153
Declaration of Independence, 148
government programs, 105-107
USSR, 72, 83, 85
and world government, 138, 140, 143-145, 158, 159, 164
and espionage, 86, 134, 135
see also Russia
U Thant, 159

Vietnam, 63, 83

Wager, W. Warren, 129
Waldheim, Kurt, 67
war
as bad, 18, 19, 20-21, 31, 80, 134, 140, 141, 158, 165
as good, 46
as inevitable, 138, 156, 159, 165, 166
preparation for, 110-111
Welles, Sumner, 142
Whitehead, Alfred North, 131
Wilson, Woodrow, 17
and the League of Nations, 19-22, 40, 42, 45, 69-70
World Bank
aims of, 94, 95
and aid to poor
as exploitive, 96-100
as good, 93-95
and debt, 100
and energy, 93-94
and foreign aid, 99
and the Third World, 93-95, 96-100
and the US, 99
as influential, 93
as supporting corrupt governments, 97, 99
profits of, 95
projects of, 94-95, 97-98
World Federalists Association, 131
world government
and conflict, 153-154, 156, 163, 166
and different government structures, 145
and economic change, 160
and federalism, 147-150, 151-154
and freedom, 146
and military power, 140, 143
and nuclear weapons, 138-141, 143, 158-160, 163, 165
and peace, 137-141, 158, 166-167
and political intervention, 146
and political situations, 134-135, 146, 156
and problems with USSR, 134, 140
and tyranny, 135-136, 140,